UGC NET : REVISED FORMAT

Library and Information Science

UGC NET : REVISED FORMAT

Library and Information Science

Volume I

OBJECTIVE

C.K. Sharma
Rakesh Kumar

ATLANTIC
PUBLISHERS & DISTRIBUTORS (P) LTD

Published by

ATLANTIC

PUBLISHERS & DISTRIBUTORS (P) LTD

7/22, Ansari Road, Darya Ganj, New Delhi-110002
Phones : +91-11-40775252, 40775214, 23273880, 23275880
Fax: +91-11-23285873
Web: www.atlanticbooks.com
E-mail: orders@atlanticbooks.com

Printed & bound in India by Atlantic Print Services

Preface

The University Grants Commission has revised its syllabus of National Eligibility Test (NET) for social and humanity disciplines. This book Library & Information Science in 3 volumes is based on the revised format of UGC NET.

Volume I contains the multiple choice questions (MCQs) of the following type:

(a) Multiple choice—tick the correct option.

(b) Matching type.

(c) True/False.

(d) Assertion-Reason type.

There will be 50 multiple choice questions. Each question will be of 2 marks (Total 100 marks).

Volume II covers Sections I and II of Paper III—which will have 4 sections.

Section I requires a candidate to write a critique of a given passage from a known thinker/writer or of a stanza from some poem of an established poet. There will be five questions asked from a given passage requiring an answer based on the contents and inferences of the passage. This Section shall carry 5 × 5 = 25 marks.

Section II requires a candidate to answer 15 questions asked across the syllabus for Paper III (Part A). The questions will be definitional or seeking particular information and are to be answered in about 30 words each. The questions in this Section shall be numbered from 6 to 20, and each question shall carry 5 marks, making a total of 5 × 15 = 75 marks.

Volume III caters to the evaluative and essay type questions asked respectively under Section III and IV of Paper III of UGC NET revised format. Structured in two sections, the book contains both brief and detailed explanation of terms related to library and information science in an alphabetical order.

In the combined form, all the three Volumes constitute an ideal book on library and information science for the aspirants of NET. It will not only enhance their knowledge of the subject but will also help them revise the known facts in a quick manner. I wish all my readers a great success in National Eligibility Test (NET).

I am very much thankful to Dr. K.R. Gupta, Chairman of Atlantic Publishers and Distributors (P) Ltd., New Delhi who found this book worth publishing.

C.K. SHARMA

Contents

VOLUME I

VOLUME II

VOLUME III

Acronyms

A

ABN	Australian Bibliographic Network
ADONIS	Article Delivery Over Network Information System
AGRIS	Agricultural Information System
AEC	Atomic Energy Commission
ALP	Advancement for Librarianship
ARIC	Agricultural Research Information Centre
AMIC	Asian Mass Communication Information Centre
ANN	Asia-Pacific News Network
ANSI	American National Standard Institute
ARPANET	Advanced Research Project Network
APINESS	Asia Pacific Information Network in Social Science

B

BANSDOC	Bangladesh National Scientific & Technical Documentation Centre
BHEL Network	Bharat Heavy Electricals Ltd., Network
BITNET	Because it is Time Network
BIOSIS	Bio Science Information Services Philadelphia
BRAIS	British Automated Information Service, U.K.
BONET	Bombay Library Network, Bombay

C

CALIBNET	Calcutta Network
CAF	Commission Appointed by Federation
CAPS	Contents, Abstract and Photocopy Service, INSDOC (1992)

CARIS	The Current Agricultural Research Information System
CARISPLAN	Caribbean Information System for Economic and Social Planning
CAS	Chemical Abstract Service
CASEARCH	Chemical Abstract Search System
CCL	Common Command Language
CDRI	Central Drug Research Institute, Lucknow
CFTRI	Central Food Technology Research Institute, Mysore
CLRI	Central Leather Research Institute, Madras
COSTI	U.S. Committee on Scientific and Technical Information
CMTI	Central Machine Tools Institute, Bangalore
CRG	Classification Research Group
CRRERIS	Commonwealth Regional Renewable Energy Resources Information System
CSIR	Council of Scientific & Industrial Research, New Delhi
CSNET	Computer Science Network, U.S.A.

D

DARDNET	Defence Advanced Research Dev. Project Network
DBMS	Database Management System
DDC	Data Dissemination Centre
DDL	Data Definition Language
DEC	Data Evaluation Centre
DELNET	Delhi Library Network
DESIDOC	Defence Science Information & Documentation Centre, New Delhi
DEVSIS	Development Science Information System
DEVINSA	Development Information Network for South Asia

DISNIC	District National Information Centre
DIS	UN Development Information System
DML	Data Manipulation Language
DRC	Data Referral Centre

E

EARN	European Academic Research Network
ENVIS	Environment Information System
EARNET	European Academic Research Network, U.K.

F

FID	International Federation for Information and Documentation

FID Advisory (Council) Groups

FID/MAG	Membership Advisory Group
FID/PR-LAG	Liaison Advisory Group

FID Regional Commissions

FID	Federation International De Documentation
FID/CAO	Commission for Asia and Oceania
FID/CLA	Commission for Latin America
FID/CNANE	Commission for Northern Africa and Near East
FID/ROE	Regional Organisation for Europe

FID Committees

FID/CR	Classification Research
FID/ET	Education and Training
FID/II	Information for Industry
FID/IPP	Information Policies and Programmes
FID/II	Intellectual in Information
FID/LI	Linguistics in Information
FID/SDI	Social Science Documentation & Information
FID/UDC	Universal Decimal Classification Consortium

FID Special Interest Group

FID/ASME	Advisory Services for Small and Medium Sized Enterprises

FID/PFI	Banking, Finance & Insurance Information
FID/EIS	Executive Information System
FID/MIP	Roles, Careers and Development of Modern Information Professional
FID/SCRM	Safety Control and Risk Management
FID/TIRM	Training for Information Resource Management
FID/EI	Environment Information
FID/IT	Information Technology
FID/IPA	Information for Public Administration
IFLA	International Federation of Library Association

IFLA Core Programmes

IFLA/UBCIM	Universal Bibliographic Control & International MARC
IFLA/UAP	Universal Availability of Publications
IFLA/PAC	Preservation and Conservation
IFLA/UDT	Universal Data Flow and Telecommunications

G

GPSS	Gateway Packet Switching Service
GSI	Geological Survey of India, Kolkata

H

HELLIS	Health, Literature, Library and Information Service

I

IAC	Information Analysis Centre
IARI	Indian Agriculture Research Institute, New Delhi
IASLIC	Indian Association of Special Library & Information Centre, Kolkata
ICAR	Indian Council of Agricultural Research
ICHR	Indian Council of Historical Research
ICMR	Indian Council of Medical Research, New Delhi

ICSSR	Indian Council of Social Science Research
IDSA	Institute of Defence Studies and Analysis, New Delhi
IFIS	International Food Information Service
ILA	Indian Library Association
IMO	Information Market Observatory, U.S.A.
IPCL	Indian Petrochemical Corporation Ltd., Vadodara
INFLIBNET	Information and Library Network (UGC)
INFLOP	Information Library Organisation Planning (Network)
INFOTERRA	International Referral System for Environment Information (UNEP)
IGCAR	Indira Gandhi Centre for Atomic Research, Kalpakkam
INIS	International Nuclear Information System
INPADOC	International Patent Documentation Centre
INSDOC	Indian National Scientific Documentation Centre, New Delhi
ISAR	Information Storage and Retrieval
ISBN	International Standard Book Number
ISBD	International Standard Bibliographical Description
ISBD(G)	International Standard Bibliographical Description (General)
ISBD(M)	International Standard Bibliographical Description (Monographs)
ISBD(S)	International Standard Bibliographical Description (Serials)
ISBD(CM)	International Standard Bibliographical Description (Cartographic Material)
ISBD(NBM)	International Standard Bibliographical Description (Non Book Material)

ISDS	International Serials Data System (UNISIST)
ISI	Institute of Scientific Information
ISONET	International Standardisation Organisation Network
ISRO	Indian Space Research Organisation, Thiruvananthapuram
ISTA	Indian Scientific Translators' Associations, INSDOC (1962)
ISSN	International Standard Serial Number
ITC	International Translation Centre, Delft, Netherlands
ITIB	Industrial and Technological Information Bank
ITRC	Industrial Toxicology Research Centre, Lucknow

J

JANET	Joint Academy Network

K

KGEU	Knowledge Generation, Exchange and Utilisation

L

LIBRIS	Swedish Library Information System
LIBSYS	Library System Software

M

MALIBNET	Madras Library Network
MAP & TOP	Manufacturing Automation Protocol and Technical and Office Protocol (U.S.A.)
MEDLINE	Medicine Library Network, USA

N

NASA	National Aeronautical Space Agency
NASSDOC	National Social Science Documentation Centre
NASSIC	National Social Science Information Centre Vadodara

NBT	National Book Trust, New Delhi
NCAER	National Centre for Aeronautics, New Delhi
NCLIS	U.S. National Commission on Library & Information Science
NICRYS	National Information Centre for Crystallography, Chennai
NIOH	National Institute of Occupational Health, Ahmedabad
NISO	National Information Standard Organisation
NISSAT	National Information System for Science & Technology, New Delhi
NML	National Medical Library
NRIEP	Nuclear Research Information Energy Programme
NTIS	U.S. National Technical Information System
NTS	National Translation Service, U.S.A.
NTPC Network	National Thermal Power Corporation Network

O

OCLC	Online Computer Library Centre, U.S.A.
OECD	Organisation for Economic Cooperation and Development
ONGC Network	Oil & Natural Gas Commission Network
OSI	Open System Interconnection

P

PADIS	Pan-American Documentation & Information System
PGI	General Information Programme
PLINLA	Planning for Lib-Org. Information Network of Latin America
POPIN	Popular Information Network, New York
PSTN	Public Switched Telephone Network
PUNENET	Puna Library Network, Pune

R

RINSCA	Regional Information Network for South & Central Asia
RLIN	Research Libraries Information Network
RRRLF	Raja Rammohan Roy Library Foundation, Kolkata

S

SAIL	Steel Authority of India Ltd.
SANDOC	Small Enterprises National Documentation Centre, Hyderabad
SIET/SENDOC	Small Industries Extension Training Institute/ Small Enterprises Documentation Centre
SNA	System Network Architecture (IBM)
SCOLAP	Scottish Library Cooperative Automation Project
SQL	Structural Query Language
SSCI	Social Science Citation Index
STSI	Scientific, Technical & Social Information
SWAL CAP	South West Academic Libraries Cooperation Automation Program

T

TERI	Tata Energy Research Institute, New Delhi
TIES	Technological Information Exchange System
TIFR	Tata Institute of Fundamental Research, Mumbai

U

UAP	Universal Availability of Publications
UGC	University Grants Commission, New Delhi
UNESCO	United Nations Educational, Scientific & Cultural Organisation
UTLIS	International: University of Toronto Library Information System

W

WAPIS — Water and Power Information System, Pune

WLS — Western Library Network (UNISIST)

X

XNS — Xerox Network System

Thesaurus Abbreviations

BT Broad Term

NT Narrower Term

RT Related Term

SN Scope Note

TT Top Term

UF Use For

USE Preferred Term

BTP Broader Term Partitive

NTG Narrower Term Generic

NTP Narrower Term Partitive

< ...... to precede broader term

< P ..... to precede a broader term

> .... to precede a Narrower term (Partitive)

= to precede a preferred term (Descriptor)

[1] to precede a Non-preferred term

- to precede a related term

Print & Non-Print Media 1

Print Media

1. Books
2. Serials
3. Pamphlets
4. Reference Books
5. Trade Literature
6. Thesis

Non-Print Media

1. Film—Photographic Film
Non-Photographic Film
2. Magnetic Tape
3. Magnetic Disc
4. Plastic Materials
5. Laser Discs
6. Optical Discs
7. CD-ROM

Formats with Medium

The Filmstrip

Slides

Cinifilm

Microform

Aparcture Card

Micro-Opaque

Microfitche

Microfilm

Splicing Sound Tape

(i) Video Tape

(ii) Video Cassettes

(iii) Open Reel
Magnetic Disc
Plastic Material

(iv) Transparent Plastic

(v) Vinyl Discs

(vi) Optical Storage Systems

Configuration

(i) Laservision

(ii) CD Audio

(iii) CD-ROM

(iv) CDV

(v) CDI

(vi) DVI

Information Technology 2

1. Impact printer includes:
   (a) Electrostatic printers (b) Laser printers
   (c) Daisy Wheel printer (d) Inkjet printer
2. The display screen attached to a terminal (VDU) has a provision for display of:
   (a) 70 characters and 24 lines per screen
   (b) 75 characters and 26 lines per screen
   (c) 80 characters and 24 lines per screen
3. Match the related term:

(a)	Single user operating system	(1) MS DOS
(b)	Multiuser operating system	(2) UNIX
(c)	Microsoft disk operation system	(3) DOS

4. Fortran, COBOL, ALGOL are the languages of:
   (a) First generation languages
   (b) Second generation languages
   (c) Third generation languages
   (d) Fourth generation languages
5. Data become information when:
   (a) Organised (b) Processed
   (c) Managed (d) Collected
6. The database CDS/ISIS has been developed and distributed by:
   (a) DESIDOC (b) NISSAT
   (c) NISCAIR (d) UNESCO

7. Match the related terms given below:

(a) Early 1950	(i) Using integrated circuits
(b) Early 1960	(ii) Based on transistor technology
(c) Early 1970	(iii) Parallel Processing System
(d) Early 1980	(iv) To handle sophisticated non-numerical application
(e) Late 1980	(v) Vacuum Tube based
(f) 1990	(vi) Development of small-scale integration

8. Which are the public data networks?
   (a) WANs (b) MANs
   (c) LANs (d) All above

9. Which is the satellite based network?
   (a) LAN (b) WAN (c) MAN

10. Match the related terms of LAN Topology given below:

(a) Star topology	(i) Connected to a bus using a passive tap
(b) Bus topology	(ii) Connected to point-to-point links between pairs of ring interface units
(c) Ring topology	(iii) Connected to a central switch

11. Match the year of origin of Ditigal networks:

(a) ISDN	(i) 1960
(b) CCITT/PCM	(ii) 1960
(c) Mini Computers	(iii) 1980

12. In which printing process impression from the plate is taken indirectly through blanket?
    (a) Plate-making process
    (b) Despatch process
    (c) Offset process

13. Unimarc was developed by:
    (a) Library of Congress (b) British Museum
    (c) Unesco (d) IFLA

14. Which format is UNESCO's General Information Programmes (PGI)?
    (a) Unimarc (b) U.K. Mark
    (c) U.S. Mark (d) CCF

15. LC launched RECON (REtrospective CONversion) Pilot in:
    (a) 1972 (b) 1968
    (c) 1969 (d) 1965

16. IBM designed:
    (a) OASIS (b) CAIRS
    (c) ISIS (d) Microlinx

17. Which integrated system is modular PC-based integrated system and designed by Dawson technology?
    (a) Librarian (b) Microlinx
    (c) OASIS (d) CAIRS

18. Which is the proper Database hierarchy in the organization of data?
    (a) Database→File→Record→Field→Character→Byte→Bit
    (b) Database→Record→File→Field→Byte→Character→Bit
    (c) Database→File→Record→Character→Field→Byte→Bit

19. Data definition part and data manipulation part are two components of:
    (a) Data hierarchical system
    (b) Data retrieval process
    (c) Database management system

20. Match the relationship of various Data models:
    (a) Hierarchical Model (i) x : m
    (b) Network Model (ii) 1 : 1
    (c) Relationship Model (iii) 1 : n

21. There were exchanges of agreements for library cooperation among the universities of Lund, Ago and Freifswald in:
    (a) 1735 (b) 1740
    (c) 1731 (d) 1742

22. The first major union list entitled "A catalogue of scientific and technical periodicals" was compiled in 1885 by:
    (a) Henry A. Sharp (b) Henry C. Bolton
    (c) Henry K. Smile (d) George Allen

23. Circuits, Message and Packet Networks are known as:
    (a) Broadcast Networks
    (b) Switched Networks
    (c) Computer Networks

24. Bhaba Atomic Research Centre (BARC), Mumbai is an operating agency of:
    (a) AGRIS (b) INIS (c) INFOTERA

25. When did DELNET begin its cooperation by inaugurating E-Mail and used E-mail 400 software?
    (a) 1990 (b) 1991
    (c) 1992 (d) 1989

26. Which multi use systems are essential for networking?
    (a) MS-DOS (b) UNIX-XENIX
    (c) Any other

27. CDS/ISIS has Export/Import facilities in:
    (a) ISO 1900 format (b) ISO 1901-2000 format
    (c) ISO 2709 format

28. Library network has which of the following characteristics?
    (a) Data, Retrieval, Access, Users
    (b) Data, Dissemination, Retrieval, Users
    (c) Data, Consolidation, Retrieval, Users

29. Management Information System (MIS) involves:
    (a) Management / System / Result
    (b) Information / Decision-making / System
    (c) Management / Information / System

30. Which metric system is applied in various statistical analyses to study pattern of authorship?
    (a) Scientometrics (b) Bebometrics
    (c) Bibliometrics

31. Which technique helps managers and decision makers to make better forcasts and advice?
    (a) Forcast Techniques (b) Delphi Techniques
    (c) L-Kart Techniques

32. "On-what" budget is also called:
    (a) Programme Budget (b) Operating Budget
    (c) Balance Sheet Budget (d) Item Budget

33. "Unit cost budget" is also called:
    (a) Capital Budget (b) Programme Budget
    (c) Performance Budget

34. There are three types of pricing:
    (a) Cost, demand and competition-based
    (b) Price, supply and product-based
    (c) Demand, supply and competition-based

35. What was the writing material about third millennium B.C.?
    (a) Clay tablets (b) Linen (c) Papyrus

36. Parchment is a writing material made from the inner side of split skin of sheep which was used:
    (a) As early as the 1500 B.C.
    (b) As early as the 1200 B.C.
    (c) As early as the 1600 B.C.

37. Paper was invented by Cai Lun in 105 AD in:
    (a) Cambodia (b) Russia (c) China

38. The first paper mill was established in America (Philadelphia) in:
    (a) 1680 (b) 1685
    (c) 1690 (d) 1692

39. Folders are publications, neither stitched nor cut and folded to make:
    (a) Two or more leaves
    (b) One or more leaves
    (c) Four or more leaves
40. Pamphlet is a non-periodical publication of at least 5 but:
    (a) Not more than 45 pages
    (b) Not more than 48 pages
    (c) Not more than 52 pages
41. "A plastic coated tape with a magnetic surface on which information can be recorded and identified by computer and other machine" is:
    (a) Magnetic drum (b) Magnetic disc
    (c) Magnetic tape
42. Which is the full form of CD-ROM?
    (a) Compact disc-Read of Memory
    (b) Complete disc-Read only Memory
    (c) Compact disc-Read only Memory
43. Identify the full form of WORM:
    (a) Work on Ready Memory
    (b) Write only Reading Memory
    (c) Write Once Read Many
44. When a document refers to another document as a source of information, it is called:
    (a) Cited document
    (b) Citing document
    (c) Citation document
45. When a document is referred by another document as a source of information, it is called:
    (a) Cited document
    (b) Citation document
    (c) Citing document

46. Identify the mathematical fourmula $1_f(Jy) = \frac{x_1 + x_2}{y_1 + y_2}$ whether applied for citation of:
   (a) Ranked list of journals by immediate index
   (b) Ranked list of journals by impact factor
   (c) Ranked list of books
47. Identify the Mathematical formula $I_i(Jy) = \frac{c}{x}$ whether applied for citation of:
   (a) Ranked list of journals by impact factor
   (b) Ranked list of journals by immediate index
   (c) Rank list of books
48. The BS (British Standard) number of UDC, Medium Edition English Text is:
   (a) BS : 1050M (b) BS : 1000M
   (c) BS : 1020M
49. The varieties of thesaurus are categorized as:
   (a) Source, construction and adjunct thesaurus
   (b) Source, adjunct and cumulative thesaurus
   (c) Cumulative, controlled and adjunct thesaurus
50. COSATI Rules were prepared for descriptive cataloguing in:
   (a) 1966 (b) 1965 (c) 1964 (d) 1962
51. Which is the correct structure of U.S. MARC format?
   (a) Leader/Directory/Control field/Variable data field
   (b) Leader/Instructions/Survey/Data structure
   (c) Leader/Directory/Control field/Variable data field
52. Which is the correct structure of U.K. Mark format?
   (a) Record Level/ Directory/ Control field/Variable data field
   (b) Record writing/Instruction/Control field/Variable data field
   (c) Record writing/Directory/Control field/Variable data field

53. Which language character is used in U.S. Mark which is established by LC and based on ALA extended version?
    (a) Alphabetic character
    (b) Symbols character
    (c) Roman character

54. UNIMARC is based on:
    (a) ISSN (b) ISBN (c) ISBD

55. Which structure of CCF record format is correct?
    (a) Record level, Directory, Data field, Record separation
    (b) Record level, Instructions, Data collection, Record separation
    (c) Record level, Guide, Data collection, Record separation

56. The chain of POPSI is made from:
    (a) Subject analysis (b) Citation analysis
    (c) Facet analysis

57. G. Bhattacharya has postulated a generalized subject indexing language with a set of categories:
    (a) Entity, Problem and Discipline with modifiers
    (b) Entity, Action and Property with modifiers
    (c) Entity, Action and Disciplines with modifiers

58. Compatibility factors and measures of ISAR systems are:
    (a) End user, Intermediary, and Data
    (b) End user, Database, and Accession
    (c) End user, Intermediary, and Raw database

59. Which is a group of models of information retrieval?
    (a) Data, Information, and Knowledge retrieval models
    (b) Data, Knowledge, and Query retrieval models
    (c) Information, Knowledge and Intellectual retrieval models

60. The process of searching information can be grouped as under:
    (a) Reference, Document, Fact, and Knowledge retrieval
    (b) Document, Problems, Reference, and Fact retrieval
    (c) Reference, Documents, Query, and Knowledge retrieval
61. How many commands the CCL (Common Command Language) consists of?
    (a) 17 commands (b) 20 commands
    (c) 30 commands (d) 24 commands
62. Which kind of knowledge is provided by libraries and information centres?
    (a) Personal knowledge (b) Individual's knowledge
    (c) Social knowledge
63. Dissection of knowledge is cutting a universe of entities into parts of coordinate status, just as we cut a slice of bread into strips:
    (a) Yes (b) No (c) Not known
64. Identify the chronological sequence of documentary sources:
    (a) Secondary sources (b) Tertiary sources
    (c) Primary sources
65. Wersig and Noveling have suggested six approaches of informations. Identify the group:
    (a) Structural, knowledge, message, meaning, effect, and process approach
    (b) Structural, message, meaning, process approach
    (c) Structural, knowledge, message, effect, and process approach
66. Brookes, a British Bibliometrician and Information Scientist has suggested the relational equation of information science. Identify the correct equation:
    (a) $K(s) + \Delta I = K(s + \Delta s)$
    (b) $K + \Delta - K(s + \Delta s)$
    (c) $K(s) + \Delta 1 - (s + \Delta s)$

67. Identify the group of basic elements of communication process:
    (a) Source → Message → Destination
    (b) Source → Data → Access
    (c) Source → Message → Access

68. Identify the correct approach group of information theory:
    (a) $V(s) = f(P_p E_{ij} V_j)$
    (b) $V = f(P_p E_{ij} V_j)$
    (c) $V(s) = (P_p E_{ij} V_j)$

69. Give the name of the information scientist who suggested the following formula of information diffusion in his book *The Science of Information*:

    $r = (ce + ci\ N(t)\ (NM - N(t)$

    (a) Chatman (b) Peter Drucker
    (c) Harlen Cleveland (d) Robert M. Losee

70. Identify the correct group of three levels for description of database architecture:
    (a) Conceptual, external, internal
    (b) Logical, external, internal
    (c) Linking, recording, internal

71. Identify [✓] the bibliographical database from among the following:
    (a) Research in progress
    (b) Chemical Abstract
    (c) CA Search
    (d) Books in print

72. Identify the correct group of components of the structure of mark format:
    (a) Leader → Record directory → Variables fields
    (b) Centre → Database → Record format
    (c) Leader → Database → Variables fields

73. Computerised cataloguing system requires at least three files:
   (a) Serial file, order file, master file
   (b) User file, master file, index file
   (c) Master file, index file, authority file
74. Computerised serial control system requires any of the following group of files:
   (a) Supplier file, serial file, order file, user file
   (b) Document file, Borrower file, user file
   (c) Supplier file, order file, document file, user file
75. Identify the group of major components of data centres:
   (a) Data source → Database → Users
   (b) Data collection → Data codification → Users
   (c) Data source → Data collection → Users
76. The Clearing House is a central agency for:
   (a) Collection, dissemination, and distribution
   (b) Collection, classification, and distribution
   (c) Collection, control, and codification
77. Which is the correct statement?
   (a) Data generation precedes data compilation
   (b) Data collection precedes data generation
   (c) Data collection precedes data retrieval
78. Which information centre have been providing reference service from Documentary sources to meet user information requirements?
   (a) Data Dissemination Centre
   (b) Data Referral Centre
   (c) Data Evaluation Centre
79. Which catalogue generally provides information for its products, branches, depots, distributors, and conditions for sale?
   (a) Trade Index (b) Trade Register
   (c) Trade Catalogue/directory

80. Which information centre is supposed to index, abstract, translate, review, synthesize, and evaluate information for data in a well-defined field of specialization?
    (a) Data Dissemination Centre
    (b) Data Evaluation Centre
    (c) Information Analysis Centre
81. *National Index of Translations*, a quarterly publication is published by:
    (a) UNESCO (b) JPRS, U.S.A.
    (c) INSDOC, India
82. Ten issues a year of *World Translation Index* (WTI), and an *Annual Index* are published by:
    (a) INSDOC India
    (b) SLA-Translation Centre, Chicago
    (c) ITC (International Translation Centre)
83. *Trade Directory of the World* is published by:
    (a) CBD Research, Beckenham
    (b) Klein Publishers, New York
    (c) Croner, New York
84. *CRC Handbook of Chemistry and Physics* has been published by:
    (a) McGraw Hill, New York
    (b) T.G. Hill, New York
    (c) Wilson, New York
    (d) CRC, Florida
85. *Statesman's Yearbook* has been published by:
    (a) C.S.O., New Delhi
    (b) Macmillan, London
    (c) U.N. Statistical Office
86. Match the related publisher of the following bulletins:
    (a) *Industrial Equipment News* (1) Arun Chamber, Bombay

(b) *Industrial Market Bulletin* (2) Thimmegowda, Bangalore

(c) *Bombay Market* (3) Balaji Publishing, Fort, Bombay

87. Match the related publishers of following International Bulletins of information products:

(a) *Machinery Market* (1) Sewell Publications, London

(b) *Product Finishing* (2) MBC Industrial Electronic Publications, Kent

(c) *Made in Europe* (3) Frankfurt, West Germany

(d) *Electrical Equipments* (4) Machinery Market, Kent, England

88. Who is the publisher of the Trend Report "Trends in Developing Economics, 1989"?

(a) FID (b) INSDOC, New Delhi

(c) World Bank, Washington

89. Name the Trend Report on Wind Energy published by INSDOC in 1982:

(a) Trends in Wind Energy

(b) Wind Energy: A Trend Report

(c) Recent Trends in Wind Energy

90. Which type of cables are widely used in long distance telephone wires and as cables for closed circuit T.V.?

(a) Twisted pair of wires (b) Coaxial cables

(c) Fiber optic cables

91. Match the year of starting the following Abstracts:

(a) Sociological Abstract, New York (1) 1927

(b) Psychological Abstract, Washington (2) 1951

(c) Education Abstract, Paris (3) 1949

(d) International Pol. Sc. Abstract, Oxford (4) 1952

92. Match the year in which the following were first introduced:

(a)	Bibliometrics	(1)	1980
(b)	Informatics	(2)	1947
(c)	Librametry	(3)	1960

93. Match the year of establishment of the following centres:

(a)	DESIDOC	(1)	1967
(b)	ICAR	(2)	1971
(c)	SANDOC	(3)	1967
(d)	OCLC	(4)	1958

94. Match the related year of introducing the following networks:

(a)	CALIBNET	(1)	1992
(b)	PUNENET	(2)	1993
(c)	ADINET	(3)	1994
(d)	MALIBNET	(4)	1988

95. Match the related year of introducing the following networks:

(a)	BONET	(1)	1995
(b)	BALNET	(2)	1988
(c)	INFLIBNET	(3)	1984
(d)	NICNET	(4)	1994

96. Match the related years of starting the Indian Abstracts mentioned below:

(a)	Indian Lib. Science Abstract	(1)	1955
(b)	Indian Education Abstract	(2)	1967
(c)	Public Administration Abstract	(3)	1972
(d)	Indian Psychological Abstract	(4)	1957

97. Match the related years of starting the Indian Abstracts mentioned below:

(a)	Indian Dissertation Abstract	(1)	1955
(b)	Physics Abstract	(2)	1970

(c) Engineering Abstract (3) 1956

(d) NBO Abstract (4) 1973

98. Match the related years of starting the Indian Abstract mentioned below:

(a) CBI Abstract (1) 1966

(b) Food Technology Abstract (2) 1965

(c) Indian Science Abstract (3) 1964

99. Match the related year of starting the Abstract as mentioned below:

(a) Chemical Abstract (U.S.A.) (1) 1926

(b) Biological Abstract (U.S.A.) (2) 1969

(c) Lib. & Inf. Sc. Abstract, Philadelphia (3) 1953

(d) Economic Abstract, Hague (4) 1907

100. Relate the manufacturer/developer of the following softwares:

(a) Library Manager (1) DESIDOC, New Delhi

(b) SUCHIKA (2) INSDOC, New Delhi

(c) GRANTHALAYA (3) NIC, Delhi

(d) TECHLIB + (4) System Data Control, Bombay

101. Relate the manufacturer/developer of the following softwares:

(a) LIBRIS (1) Algorithms, Pune

(b) SLIM (2) Tata Unisys, Bangalore

(c) TULIPS (3) Wipro, Bangalore

(d) WILSYS (4) Frontier Inf. Tech. Hyderabad

102. Relate the manufacturer/developer of the following softwares:

(a) LIBSOFT (1) CMC Ltd., Calcutta

(b) MAITRAYEE (2) Soft Aid, Poona

(c) LIBRARIAN (3) Uptron India, New Delhi

(d) SALIM (4) ET&T, New Delhi

103. Match the related years of introducing the following classification schemes:

(a) LC Classification Scheme	(1) 1933
(b) Colon Classification	(2) 1949-53
(c) Bibliographical Classification	(3) 1920
(d) Lib. Biblio-Classification (BBK-USSR)	(4) 1904

104. Match the related locations of the following organisations:

(a) DRTC	(1) 1986
(b) ICMR	(2) 1983
(c) NCSI	(3) 1946
(d) UNESCO	(4) Bangalore

105. Match the related years of the following conferences and symposiums:

(a) ICCP, Paris	(1) 1969
(b) IMCE, Copenhagen	(2) 1978
(c) ISBEF, Taormina	(3) 1961

106. Match the related years of the following systems/formats:

(a) CCF	(1) 1987
(b) CCL	(2) 1950
(c) Coordinate indexing	(3) 1968-69
(d) PRECIS	(4) 1984

107. Match the related year of introducing of the reprographics:

(a) Microform	(1) 1972
(b) Micro publishing	(2) 1970
(c) Microfilm reader (Portable)	(3) 1960
(d) Telegraphy	(4) 1937

MATCHING QUESTIONS

108. Match the related place of location of the following journals:

(a) *Herald of Library Science*	(1) Chicago
(b) *IASLIC Bulletin*	(2) Lucknow
(c) *ILA Bulletin*	(3) Calcutta
(d) *Library Quarterly*	(4) Delhi

109. Match the related place of location of the following references sources:

(a) *Manorama Year Book*	(1) Calcutta
(b) *International Library Review*	(2) Paris
(c) *UNISIST News Letter*	(3) London
(d) *Granthalaya*	(4) Kottayam

110. Relate the name of the author of the undermentioned books:

(a) *Elements of Library Classification*	(1) Dr. C.K. Sharma
(b) *Library Administration: Theory and Practice*	(2) B. Guha
(c) *University Library: Organisation and Management*	(3) R.L. Mittal
(d) *Documentation and Information*	(4) Dr. S.R. Ranganathan

111. Relate the names of author of undermentioned books:

(a) *Fundamentals of Documentation*	(1) D. Davison
(b) *Towards Paperless Information System*	(2) Dr. C.K. Sharma
(c) *Soochna Pradhyogiki*	(3) F.W. Lancaster
(d) *Bibliographic Control*	(4) P.S. Kwatra

112. Relate the names of author of undermentioned books:

(a)	*Five Laws of Library Science*	(1)	Dr. C.K. Sharma
(b)	*Information Science*	(2)	Dr. S.R. Ranganathan
(c)	*Library & Culture*	(3)	Dr. S.R. Ranganathan
(d)	*Prolegomence to Library Classification*	(4)	R.C. Benge

113. Match the year of enactment of Public Library Act of the State:

(a)	Tamil Nadu	(1)	1989
(b)	Andhra Pradesh	(2)	1965
(c)	Maharashtra	(3)	1967
(d)	Karnataka	(4)	1960
(e)	Kerala	(5)	1948

114. Match the persons with their contributions:

(a)	Chain Indexing	(1)	J.R. Sharp
(b)	Thesaurus	(2)	Minni Eaal Sears
(c)	Subject Indexing	(3)	P.M. Roget
(d)	SLIC Indexing	(4)	M. Taub
(e)	Unitern Indexing	(5)	S.R. Ranganathan

115. Match the place of Headquarters of the Associations:

(a)	Library Association	(1)	Delhi
(b)	Indian Library Association	(2)	The Hague
(c)	IFLA	(3)	Kolkata
(d)	IASLIC	(4)	New Delhi
(e)	GILA	(5)	London

116. Match the starting of publication with the Associations:

(a)	UDC	(1)	1933
(b)	CC	(2)	1935
(c)	BC	(3)	1876
(d)	DDC	(4)	1961
(e)	RIC	(5)	1905

ANSWERS—INFORMATION TECHNOLOGY

1. (c) Daisy Wheel Printer
2. (c) 80 characters and 24 lines per screen
3. a/3
4. (d) Fourth generation language
5. (b) Processed
6. (d) UNESCO
7. a/5, b/2, c/1, d/6, e/3, f/4
8. (d) All above
9. (b) WAN
10. a/3, b/1, c/2
11. a/3, b/1, c/2
12. (c) Offset process
13. (d) IFLA
14. (d) CCF
15. (c) 1969
16. (d) Microlinx
17. (c) OASIS
18. (a) Data→File→Record→Field→Character→Byte→Bit
19. (c) Database Management System
20. a/3, b/1, c/2
21. (b) 1740
22. (b) Henry C. Bolton
23. (b) Switched Networks
24. (b) INIS
25. (b) 1991
26. (b) UNIX-XENIX
27. (c) ISO 2709 format
28. (a) Data, Retrieval, Access, Users
29. (c) Management / Information / System
30. (c) Bibliometrics

31. (b) Delphi Techniques
32. (d) Item Budget
33. (c) Performance Budget
34. (a) Cost, demand and competition-based
35. (c) Papyrus
36. (a) As early as the 1500 BC
37. (c) China
38. (c) 1690
39. (a) Two or more leaves
40. (b) Not more than 48 pages
41. (c) Magnetic tapes
42. (c) Compact Disc-Read Only Memory
43. (c) Write Once Ready Many
44. (b) Citing document
45. (a) Cited document
46. (b) Ranked list of journals by impact factor
47. (b) Ranked list of journals by immediate index
48. (d) BS:1000M
49. (b) Source, adjunct, and cumulative thesaurus
50. (a) 1966
51. (a) Leader/Directory/Control field/Variable data field
52. (a) Record level/Directory/Control field/Variable data field
53. (c) Roman character
54. (c) ISBD
55. (a) Record level, Directory, Data field, Record separation
56. (c) Facet Analysis
57. (b) Entity, Action, and Property with modifiers
58. (c) End user, Intermediary, and Raw database
59. (a) Data, Information, and Knowledge retrieval models
60. (a) Reference, Document, Fact, and Knowledge retrieval
61. (b) 20 commands

62. (c) Social Knowledge
63. (a) Yes
64. (c) (a) (b) Primary → Secondary → Tertiary
65. (a) Structure, knowledge, message, meaning, effect and process
66. (c) K (s) + Δ1 - (s + Δs)
67. (b) Source → Data → Access
68. (a) $V(s) = f(P_p\ E_{ij}\ V_j)$
69. (d) Robert M. Losee
70. (a) Conceptual, external, internal
71. c, d—CA Search, Books in print
72. (a) Leader, Record Directory, Variable field
73. (b) Master file, index file, authority file
74. (a) Supplier file, serial file, order file, user file
75. (a) Data source → Database → Users
76. (b) Collection, Classification and Distribution
77. (a) Data generation precedes data compilation
78. (b) Data Referral Centre
79. (c) Trade Catalogue/Directory
80. (c) Information Analysis Centre
81. (c) INSDOC
82. (c) ITC (International Translation Centre)
83. (c) Croner, New York
84. (d) CRC, Florida
85. (b) Macmillan, London
86. a/3, b/2, c/1
87. a/4, b/1, c/3, d/2
88. (c) World Bank, Washington
89. (c) Recent trends in wind energy
90. (b) Coaxial cables
91. a/4, b/1, c/3, d/2

92. a/3, b/1, c/3
93. a/4, b/1, c/2, d/3
94. a/4, b/1, c/2, d/3
95. a/4, b/1, c/2, d/3
96. a/2, b/1, c/4, d/3
97. a/4, b/1, c/2, d/3
98. a/3, b/1, c/2
99. a/4, b/1, c/2, d/3
100. a/4, b/1, c/2, d/3
101. a/4, b/1, c/2, d/3
102. a/4, b/1, c/2, d/3
103. a/4, b/1, c/2, d/3
104. a/4, b/1, c/2, d/3
105. a/3, b/1, c/2
106. a/4, b/1, c/2, d/3
107. a/3, b/1, c/2, d/4

MATCHING ANSWERS

108. a/2, b/3, c/4, d/1
109. a/4, b/3, c/2, d/1
110. a/4, b/3, c/1, d/2
111. a/4, b/3, c/2, d/1
112. a/2, b/1, c/4, d/3
113. a/5, b/4, c/3, d/2, e/1
114. a/5, b/1, c/2, d/3, e/4
115. a/5, b/1, c/2, d/3, e/4
116. a/5, b/1, c/2, d/3, e/4

FILL IN THE BLANKS

1. Henri La Fountain was awarded Nobel Prize in the year............
   (a) 1910 (b) 1911 (c) 1912 (d) 1913

2. The UGC Library Committee under the Chairmanship of Dr. S.R. Ranganathan was constituted in......
   (a) 1950 (b) 1952 (c) 1954 (d) 1956
3. OCLC is network:
   (a) Online (b) Offline (c) Both of these
4. INSDOC was established at New Delhi in......
   (a) 1950 (b) 1951 (c) 1952 (d) 1953
5. *University Handbook* is published by AIU, New Delhi......
   (a) Every year (b) Every two years
   (c) Every five years
6. INSDOC is publishing......
   (a) Indian Physics Abstract
   (b) Indian Science Abstract
   (c) Indian Psychological Abstract
7. The Headquarter of Special Library Association (U.S.A.) is at....
   (a) Washington (b) New York (c) Michigan
8. Before independence National Library of India was known as....
   (a) Royal Library
   (b) Calcutta Library
   (c) Imperial Library
9. National Library week is organized every year in India in the month of......
   (a) July (b) August
   (c) September (d) October
   (e) November
10. INFLIBNET is an unit of......
    (a) ICSSR (b) ICMR
    (c) UGC (d) NASSDOC
11. IFLA was founded in the year......
    (a) 1921 (b) 1923 (c) 1925 (d) 1927

12. Videotext is an example of......
    (a) Print media (b) Non-print media
    (c) Electronic media
13. The journal *Library Science with Slant to Documentation* Bangalore changed its title from......
    (a) Vol. 21, 1994 (b) Vol. 23, 1996
    (c) Vol. 25, 1998 (d) Vol. 27, 2000
14. The Editor of the *Journal of Library and Information Technology* is......
    (a) P.N. Wahi (b) S. Kumar
    (c) Dr. C.K. Sharma (d) M.P. Sinha
15. *Bibliography of Bibliographies* is a......of information.
    (a) Primary source (b) Secondary source
    (c) Tertiary source
16. *University News* New Delhi is published by...........
    (a) UPLA (b) ILA (c) AIU (d) IASLIC
17. IASLIC, Kolkata is publishing...........
    (a) Indian Science Abstract
    (b) Indian Library Science Abstract
    (c) Indian Information Abstract
18. Conrad Gesner is known as father of...........
    (a) Documentation (b) Reference Service
    (c) Bibliography (d) Information Service
19. Mr. J.P. Cowarani was the Editor of DDC...........
    (a) 18th edition (b) 19th edition
    (c) 20th edition (d) 21st edition
20. 'Racial, Ethenic and National Group' in DDC is a...........
    (a) Table 7 (b) Table 6
    (c) Table 5 (d) Table 4
21. The 3rd volume of DDC (19th ed.) is called ....
    (a) Index (b) Special Index
    (c) Comprehensive Index (d) Relative Index

22. 'Schedules' in colon classification is a......
    (a) Part 1 (b) Part 2 (c) Part 3
23. M.A. Gopinath edited the......of colon classification:
    (a) Edition 3 (b) Edition 5
    (c) Edition 6 (d) Edition 7
24. Five Fundamental Categories in CC are.........
    (a) DMRST (b) PREST (c) PMEST (d) RCEST
25. The size of standard catalogue card is.........
    (a) 11.5 × 7cm (b) 12 × 7.5cm
    (c) 12.5 × 7.5cm
26. There are two kinds of Abstracts, viz. Informative and.....
    (a) Logical (b) Possessive
    (c) Indicative
27. The Unitern indexing system was developed by:
    (a) IFLA (b) M. Taub
    (c) G. Denton (d) UNISIST
28. CCF is a Universal Exchange format for:
    (a) Bibliographic record (b) Cataloguing system
    (c) Classification purpose
29. ISSN (International Standard Serial Number) consists of........
    (a) Eight digits (b) Nine digits
    (c) Ten digits (d) Eleven digits
30. The first exhaustive and extensive test of ISAR was carried at:
    (a) Lisbon (b) New York (U.S.A.)
    (c) Cranfield (U.K.) (d) Paris
31. There are two types of the Internet Browsers, viz. Text based and.........
    (a) Graphic user interface (b) Document based
    (c) Index based
32. ....Network is often called as Remote Login.
    (a) JANET (b) NICNET (c) TELNET

33. We put the right person at right place (job) in the...... system.
    (a) Financing (b) Budgeting
    (c) Managing (d) Staffing

34. The acronym POSDCORB stands for the element of......
    (a) Financial Process (b) Personnel Process
    (c) Management Process (d) Organisational Process

35. S.R. Ranganathan introduced.........for recording of periodicals.
    (a) Single card system (b) Two card system
    (c) Three card system (d) No card system

36. The Librarian generally acts as............in the Library Committee:
    (a) Chairman (b) Member
    (c) Convener/Member Secretary (d) Vice-Chairman

37. Zero based budgeting was developed by...........
    (a) A. Maslow (b) G.E. Evans
    (c) P. Phyor (d) L. Brandes

38. ....expounded MBO in his book entitled *The Practice of Management*.
    (a) George Huber (b) Peter F. Drucker
    (c) L.F. Urwick (d) Brown

39. ....suggested three performance criteria for library service, viz. Quality, Time and Cost.
    (a) J. Brown (b) S.R. Ranganathan
    (c) F.W. Lancaster (d) M. Philips

40. IFLA launched two new programmes, viz. Universal Data Flow and preservation and conservation in the year.............
    (a) 1985 (b) 1986 (c) 1987 (d) 1988

41. MARC was developed by...........
    (a) FID (b) NISCAIR
    (c) IFLA (d) UNESCO

42. UNISIST Programmes was launched by ....
    (a) IFLA (b) UNISIST
    (c) UNESCO (d) NIC
43. Which Indian Software was developed by NISCAIR based on CDS/ISIS ....?
    (a) INFLIBNET (b) GRANTHALAYA
    (c) SANJAY (d) VIDYA
44. UK MARK is developed on analogy of ....
    (a) UNIMARC (b) CCF (c) US MARC
45. INFLIBNET introduced COPSAT Service to libraries in the year...........
    (a) 1991 (b) 1992 (c) 1993 (d) 1994

ANSWERS—FILL IN THE BLANKS

1. (d) 1913
2. (b) 1952
3. (a) Online
4. (c) 1952
5. (a) Every year
6. (b) Indian Science Abstract
7. (b) New York
8. (c) Imperial Library
9. (c) November
10. (c) UGC
11. (d) 1927
12. (c) Electronic Media
13. (c) Vol. 25, 1998
14. (c) Dr. C.K. Sharma
15. (c) Tertiary Sources
16. (c) AIU
17. (b) Indian Library Science Abstract
18. (c) Bibliography

19. (c) 20th edition
20. (c) Table 5
21. (d) Relative Index
22. (b) Part 2
23. (d) Edition 7
24. (c) PMEST
25. (c) 12.5 × 7.5cm
26. (c) Indicative
27. (b) M. Taub
28. (a) Bibliographic record
29. (b) Nine Digits
30. (c) Cranfield (UK)
31. (a) Graphic user interface
32. (c) TELNET
33. (d) Staffing
34. (c) Management Process
35. (c) Three card system
36. (c) Convener/Member Secretary
37. (c) P. Phyor
38. (b) Peter F. Drucker
39. (c) F.W. Lancaster
40. (b) 1986
41. (c) IFLA
42. (c) UNESCO
43. (c) SANJAY
44. (c) US MARC
45. (c) 1993

General Questions 3

1. *Herald of Library Science* is published from:
   (a) Delhi (b) Varanasi
   (c) Lucknow (d) Kolkata
2. The Headquarter of Raja Ram Mohan Roy Library Foundation (RRRLF) is at:
   (a) Kolkata (b) Mumbai
   (c) New Delhi (d) Patna
3. India Office is located at:
   (a) Kolkata (b) London
   (c) Mumbai (d) Manchester
4. The Headquarter of UNESCO is at:
   (a) London (b) New York
   (c) Paris (d) Rome
5. The author of *Introduction to Librarianship* is:
   (a) R.N. Lock (b) J.K. Gates
   (c) M. George (d) L. Carnovsky
6. IFLA's International Office for Universal Bibliographic control is located at:
   (a) New York (b) Paris
   (c) London (d) Montreal
7. VINITY is National Documentation Centre of:
   (a) Poland (b) Hungary
   (c) Spain (d) Russia
8. Who is the author of *Communication, Knowledge and Librarian*?
   (a) L. Liberto (b) K.J. McGary
   (c) J.E. Jones (d) F. Machlup

9. CAS and SDI are examples of:
   (a) Search Service (b) Technical Enquiry
   (c) Alerting Service (d) Document Delivery Service

10. How many public libraries receive books under Delivery of Books and Newspapers Act, 1954 in India?
    (a) One (b) Two (c) Three (d) Four

11. Indian Library Association regularly brings out:
    (a) Bulletin (b) Newsletter
    (c) News Digest

12. *Indian Library Science Abstracts* is being brought out by:
    (a) UPLA (b) ILA (c) INSDOC (d) AISLIC

13. Sir Anthony Pannizzi was associated with:
    (a) Library of Congress (b) British Museum
    (c) VINITY (d) National Library, India

14. The publisher of *Reader's Guide to Periodical Literature* is:
    (a) Macmillan (b) McGraw Hill
    (c) Wilson & Co. (d) Oxford

15. The National output centre for AGRIS in India is:
    (a) ARIC (b) ICAR (c) NIRD (d) ICMR

16. *World of Learning* published by Europa Publications was started in:
    (a) 1945 (b) 1947 (c) 1950 (d) 1951

17. Which is the present body of NASSDOC?
    (a) ICHR (b) ICSSR
    (c) ICMR (d) IARI

18. The Indian Press Index is published by:
    (a) ILA (b) IASLIC
    (c) Panjab Library Association
    (d) Delhi Library Association

19. Who is the publisher of Index Translationum?
    (a) UNO (b) FAO
    (c) UNIDO (d) UNESCO

20. Who was the Editor of Webster's *Third New International Dictionary*?
    (a) M. Robinson (b) G.C. Merriam
    (c) Longman (d) Oxford

21. *World of Learning* is an:
    (a) Almanac (b) Dictionary
    (c) Directory (d) Encyclopedia

22. Who is the publisher of *Books in Print*?
    (a) ASLIB (b) UNESCO
    (c) R.R. Bowker (d) Macmillan

23. The *Asian Recorder* is published by:
    (a) Grollier (b) Marcel Dekker
    (c) K.K. Thomas (d) Academic Press

24. Who is the publisher of *Encyclopedia Americana*?
    (a) Grollier (b) Marcel Dekker
    (c) Macmillan (d) Grover

25. WWW is multimedia linked database system that spans:
    (a) Globe (b) Asia
    (c) North America (d) Europe

26. The person who propounded 'One Place Theory' in classification is:
    (a) Cutter (b) Dewey (c) Brown (d) Bliss

27. Asterisk symbol * is used in 7th ed. of CC to indicate:
    (a) Common Isolate (b) Phase edition
    (c) Speciator

28. In which year MARC-2 was launched by LC?
    (a) 1967 (b) 1968 (c) 1969 (d) 1970

29. Subject headings and thesauri are which type of indexing language?
    (a) Free (b) Natural
    (c) Conventional (d) Controlled

30. Who formulated Uniterm Indexing?
    (a) D. Austin (b) B.C. Vickery
    (c) F.W. Lancaster (d) M. Taub

31. Which of the following is not coordinate indexing?
    (a) Classified Index (b) PRECIS
    (c) POPSI (d) UNITERM
32. Which system considers the name of authors as keywords?
    (a) KWIC (b) KWOC
    (c) POPSI (d) PRECIS
33. The concept of "Systematic Indexing" was developed by:
    (a) E.J. Coats (b) B.C. Vickery
    (c) K.D. Carlyle (d) J.E.L. Farradane
34. The idea of Auto Index was given by:
    (a) Derek Austin (b) H.P. Luhn
    (c) V.C. Vickery (d) F.W. Lancaster
35. In which cataloguing code, the name of series is rendered in main entry in Note Section:
    (a) CCC (b) AARC-II (c) LC system
36. In which catalogue code rules are provided to render tracing section in the back of main entry:
    (a) AACR-II (b) CCC
37. Which is the indicator symbol for statement of responsibility?
    (a) Dot (b) Slash (c) Semicolon (d) Colon
38. The catalogue code which recognizes the "Principal Author" is:
    (a) CCC (b) AACR-II
    (c) Vatican Code
39. In which catalogue code ISBN number is given in main entry?
    (a) AACR (b) AACR-II
    (c) CCC (d) ALA
40. Which canon is known as Master Canon of Cataloguing in CCC?
    (a) Canon of Individualisation
    (b) Canon of Sought heading

(c) Canon of Recall value

(d) Canon of Ascertainability

41. Brown Issue System was devised by:

(a) Nina Brown (b) R.J. Brown
(c) A.J. Brown (d) J.D. Brown

42. Who introduced the concept of MBO (Management By Objective)?

(a) P. Drucker (b) H. Fayal
(c) L. Brandes (d) L. Spino

43. Shelflist is useful for:

(a) Stock taking (b) Stock rectification
(c) Accessioning (d) Ordering

44. In which book Ranganathan suggested staff formula:

(a) *Five Laws of Library Science*

(b) *Library Administration*

(c) *Library Manual*

45. Who enunciated the 'two factor theory of motivation'?

(a) F. Herzberg (b) E. Mayo
(c) A. Mansfield (d) McLean

46. Who enunciated the principle of "The best book to the largest number at least cost":

(a) Drury (b) Dewey
(c) Ranganathan (d) McColvin

47. ISO 9000 is one of the most widely recognized quality tool for:

(a) Administration (b) Organisation
(c) Management (d) Reference Service

48. E mail is delivered through:

(a) Speed post (b) Air-mail
(c) Mini Computer (PC)

49. Which organization developed 'Sanjay Software'?

(a) UNESCO (b) NASSDOC
(c) NISCAIR (d) DESIDOC

50. Which network is primarily concerned with academic activities?
    (a) ERNET (b) INFLIBNET
    (c) NICNET (d) DELNET

51. SENDOC was established primarily to cater to the information need of:
    (a) Large Industries
    (b) Small Scale Industries
    (c) Private Industries

ANSWERS—GENERAL QUESTION

1. (c) Lucknow
2. (b) Mumbai
3. (b) London
4. (c) Paris
5. (b) J.K. Gates
6. (b) Paris
7. (d) Russia
8. (b) K.J. McGary
9. (c) Alerting Service
10. (d) Four
11. (a) Bulletin
12. (d) AISLIC
13. (b) British Museum
14. (c) Wilson & Co.
15. (a) ARIC
16. (b) 1947
17. (b) ICSSR
18. (d) Delhi Lib. Association
19. (d) UNESCO
20. (c) Longman
21. (b) Directory
22. (c) R.R. Bowker
23. (c) K.K. Thomas
24. (a) Grollier
25. (a) Globe
26. (c) Brown
27. (c) Speciator
28. (c) 1969
29. (d) Controlled
30. (d) M. Taub
31. (d) UNITERM
32. (b) KWOC
33. (d) J.E.L. Farradane
34. (b) H.P. Luhn
35. (a) CCC
36. (b) CCC
37. (b) Slash
38. (b) AACR-II
39. (b) AACR-II
40. (c) Canon of Recall Value
41. (a) Nina Brown
42. (a) P. Drucker

43. (a) Stock taking
44. (b) Lib. Administration
45. (a) F. Herzberg
46. (b) Dewey
47. (c) Management
48. (c) Mini Computer (PC)
49. (c) NISCAIR
50. (b) INFLIBNET
51. (b) Small Scale Industries

Classification

4

1. Which scheme is the basis of UDC?
   (a) LC Classification Scheme
   (b) Knowledge Classification
   (c) Dewey Decimal Classification
2. Universal Decimal Classification is extended for use in classifying?
   (a) Periodicals, monographs, documents
   (b) Monographs, documents
   (c) Periodicals, documents
3. The full English Edition of UDC has been published as:
   (a) B.S. 1000 (b) B.S. 100 (c) B.S. 500
4. The abridged edition B.S. 1000A was first published in:
   (a) 1947 (b) 1948 (c) 1949
5. The abridged edition B.S. 1000A was based on:
   (a) Official Dutch abridgement 1946
   (b) Official Dutch abridgement 1947
   (c) Official Dutch abridgement 1948
6. Which abridged edition of UDC is called the International Standard abridged edition?
   (a) First edition (b) Second edition
   (c) None of these
7. The appearance of a zero in a DC number usually means that the subject represented by the preceding digits is divided by:
   (a) Principle of form of presentation
   (b) Principle of division
   (c) Principle of editing

8. The flexibility of the UDC lies in its use of:
   (a) Symbolic language (b) Schedule
   (c) Auxiliary numbers
9. Universal Decimal Classification is based on the principle of proceeding:
   (a) From general to specific
   (b) From specific to general
   (c) From specific to specific
10. Logical classification seldom requires regular step by step subdivision into:
    (a) 10 (b) 9 (c) 0
11. Auxiliaries in Universal Decimal Classification eliminates:
    (a) Grouping of one fact (b) Repetition
    (c) Individualisation
12. Auxiliaries in Universal Decimal Classification do not stand:
    (a) Alone
    (b) For division of subjects
    (c) None of them
13. More than one auxiliary (UDC) is seldom necessary especially when applied in conjunction with the sign:
    (a) Colon (:) (b) Comma (,)
    (c) Fullstop (.)
14. Which common isolates are provided with double signs ( ) and " "—
    (a) Name (b) Subject (c) Place, Time
15. Which is a relation sign in Universal Decimal Classification?
    (a) ; (semicolon) (b) : (colon)
    (c) — (dash)
16. Which sign is used for common auxiliaries of language in UDC?
    (a) — (Dash) (b) = (parallel) (c) : (semicolon)

17. Do you agree that classification is a/an:
    (a) Methodological distribution of classes
    (b) Arranging procedure of classes
    (c) Systematic division of classes
18. The infinite universe is:
    (a) Growing universe
    (b) Finite number of entities
    (c) Qualitative measure of an entity
19. The arrays are:
    (a) The classes of a single characteristic in one step
    (b) The classes of a more than one characteristic in one step
    (c) The classes of a single characteristic in more than one step
20. An array is:
    (a) Sequence of a class made up of any given classes
    (b) Sequence of a class made up of any given class
    (c) Sequence of classes made up of many given classes
21. Classifier is a person who:
    (a) Constructs a scheme of classification
    (b) Categorises a scheme of classification
    (c) Designs a scheme of classification
22. Classifier is a person who:
    (a) Classifies the library
    (b) Classifies the library universe
    (c) Classifies the library documents
23. Which type of subject has a basic class and one or more isolate ideas as components?
    (a) Complex subject (b) Single subject
    (c) Compound subject
24. Which subject is of greater extension and small intension?
    (a) Micro subject (b) Compound subject
    (c) Macro subject

25. Which subject is of small extension and great intension?
    (a) Large subject (b) Macro subject
    (c) Micro subject

26. What will you call a term used to denote any component, be it a basic subject, or isolate or a compound subject?
    (a) Focus (b) Isolate (c) Facet

27. Identify the author of *Organisation of Knowledge in Libraries* published in 1933?
    (a) E.C. Richardson (b) Berwick Sayers
    (c) H.E. Bliss

28. Who formulated the fundamental principles of classification called 'criteria'?
    (a) H.E. Bliss (b) E.C. Richardson
    (c) S.R. Ranganathan

29. Identify the author of the book *Classification, Theoretical and Practical* in 1901?
    (a) E.C. Richardson (b) S.R. Ranganathan
    (c) J.S. Mill

30. When did Dr. Ranganathan go on observation tour of the U.K.?
    (a) 1932 (b) 1924 (c) 1927

31. Identify the publisher of the book *Prolegomena to Library Classification* of Dr. S.R. Ranganathan?
    (a) 1936 (b) 1937 (c) 1938

32. Who used word 'canon' in book *Manual of Classification* in 1926?
    (a) S.R. Ranganathan (b) W.C. Berwick Sayers
    (c) C.A. Cutter

33. In which 'Principle of Helpful Sequence' are subjects or isolates arranged parallel to their evolution?
    (a) Principle of Later-in-Evolution
    (b) Principle of Evolution-in-Time
    (c) Later-in-Evolution principle

34. Which 'plane' represents ideas in words?
    (a) Idea plane (b) Notational plane
    (c) Verbal plane

35. Which term is defined as 'the system of terms' by S.R. Ranganathan?
    (a) Class terms (b) Terminology
    (c) Vocabulary (d) Thesaurus

36. What will be the 'order' or sequence of homonym in Biology?
    (a) Class-order-family-genus-species
    (b) Class-family-order-species-genus
    (c) Class-order-genus-family-species

37. How many canons come under 'canons of terminology'?
    (a) 2 (b) 3 (c) 4 (d) 5

38. What term is used for a single isolated primary symbol occurring in a notational system?
    (a) Isolate (b) Facet (c) Digit

39. Which term is defined by Ranganathan as "a system of ordinal numbers used to represent the classes in a scheme of classification"?
    (a) Notational plane (b) Class numbers
    (c) Notations

40. Which type of notations are used in DDC?
    (a) Mixed notations (b) Pure notations

41. Which are multi-partite notations?
    (a) Pure notations (b) Mixed notations
    (c) Focus notations (d) Faceted notations

42. In which year Dewey used Decimal fraction notation in Library Classification?
    (a) 1874 (b) 1876 (c) 1878 (d) 1902

43. Which device increases the capacity of notation in any array?
    (a) Sector device (b) Octave device
    (c) Group notation device

44. From which language is the word 'Mnemonic' originated?
    (a) Latin (b) Greek (c) French

45. Mnemonic is defined as:
    (a) The art of assisting memory
    (b) The art of assigning memory
    (c) The system of keeping in memory

46. How many kinds of notation have been introduced by Dr. Ranganathan ?
    (a) Two (b) Three
    (c) Four (d) Five

47. Which type of Mnemonics have been defined as 'literary Mnemonics' by Bliss?
    (a) P-scheduled Mnemonics (b) Seminal Mnemonics
    (c) Alphabetical Mnemonics

48. Which term is given by Berwick Sayers to the 'Hospitality of Notations' of Dr. Ranganathan?
    (a) Expensiveness
    (b) Flexibility of notation
    (c) Quality of notations

49. Which device is called when some digits are left unused at both the ends of array?
    (a) Mixed Base Device (b) Sectorising digit
    (c) Gap device

50. How many fundamental categories are devised by Dr. Ranganathan?
    (a) 3 (b) 4 (c) 5

51. In which year did J.D. Brown originate the 'The Subject Classification'?
    (a) 1898 (b) 1899 (c) 1901 (d) 1902

52. Identify the author of *Classification and Indexing in Science* and *Faceted Classification*?
    (a) Berwick Sayer (b) H.E. Bliss
    (c) B.C. Vickery

53. Whenever bare digit z is not implied by Geographical device or by Alphabetical device, which type of common isolates are used to form main class of Generalia?
    (a) Anteriorising common isolates
    (b) Chronological class
    (c) Neither of them
54. Which edition of colon classification is known as Almost Freely Faceted Classification?
    (a) Edition 4 to Edition 5
    (b) Edition 3 to Edition 7
    (c) Edition 4 to Edition 6
    (d) Edition 7
55. In which year was the first edition of colon classification published?
    (a) 1931 (b) 1932 (c) 1933 (d) 1934
56. What is the full name of Melvil Dewey?
    (a) Melville Kossuth Dewey
    (b) Melville Kossuth Louis Dewey
    (c) Melvil Louis Kossuth Dewey
57. What is the title of the DC first published in 1876?
    (a) *A Classification of Subject*
    (b) *A Classification of Subject Index*
    (c) *A Classification and Subject Index*
58. In which year Melvil Dewey joined as First Manager of 'Library Bureau'?
    (a) 1881 (b) 1882 (c) 1884
59. From which year have DC numbers been printed on LC printed cards?
    (a) 1928 (b) 1929 (c) 1930
60. In which year DC numbers started being used for arrangement of British National Bibliography?
    (a) 1948 (b) 1949 (c) 1950

61. For which division of knowledge was 'O' used in DC?
    (a) Philosophy (b) General History
    (c) Generalities

62. In which edition DC used concept of form division for the first time?
    (a) 2nd edition (b) 3rd edition
    (c) 1st edition

63. How many volumes are in 21st edition of DC?
    (a) Two (b) Three (c) Four (d) Five

64. Which division represents a recurring physical form or approach and applicable to all subjects?
    (a) Relative Index (b) Standard subdivisions

65. Which area represents historical periods and persons?
    (a) Individual language area
    (b) Group of persons area
    (c) Geographical area

66. Which classification scheme provided foundation for the development of UDC?
    (a) LC (b) DDC (c) BC

67. What was the profession of Paul Otlet (1869-1944) before taking the project of Universal Bibliographic Repertory?
    (a) Lawyer (b) Barrister
    (c) Judge (d) Librarian

68. For what purpose did Paul Otlet and Henri La Fontaine translate DC in France?
    (a) For expensibility (b) Bibliographical use
    (c) Translation purpose

69. What is the name of first publication known as first edition of UDC?
    (a) *Handbook of Universal Bibliographic Repertory*
    (b) *Handbook of Bibliographic Index*

70. In which year the first edition of UDC was published?
    (a) 1904-1907 (b) 1901-1905 (c) 1904-1906
71. How many subdivisions were included in first edition of UDC?
    (a) 33000 subdivisions (b) 33500 subdivisions
    (c) 34500 subdivisions
72. In which year was the second edition of UDC published?
    (a) 1927-33 (b) 1925-32 (c) 1925-35
73. What was the title of second edition of UDC?
    (a) *Decimal Classification Universalle*
    (b) *Classification Decimal Universalle*
    (c) *Universalle Decimal Classification*
74. In which language was the third edition of UDC published?
    (a) French (b) German (c) English
75. In which year was UDC adopted by United Kingdom?
    (a) 1927 (b) 1928 (c) 1929
76. When was the first Abridged edition of UDC in English published?
    (a) 1947 (b) 1948 (c) 1949 (d) 1950
77. What followed 4th full English edition as BS 1000 of UDC?
    (a) BSIB and ASLIB
    (b) Science Museum Library and ASLIB
    (c) HM Stationary Office and BSIB
78. Which of the following is a centre for the management and maintenance of UDC?
    (a) IFLA (b) ASLIB (c) FID
79. In how many languages has UDC been published?
    (a) 22 languages (b) 23 languages
    (c) 24 languages

80. What is the nomenclature of the committee of UDC which was given responsibility for development and maintenance of UDC?
    (a) Classification Committee
    (b) Central Classification Committee
    (c) Classification Central Committee
81. How many kinds of symbols are used in common auxiliaries of UDC?
    (a) Two (b) Three (c) Four
82. How many parts is CC7 comprised of?
    (a) 3 Parts (b) 4 Parts (c) 5 Parts (d) 6 Parts
83. What is the full form of CRG, London?
    (a) Contribution of Classification Research Group
    (b) Classification Research Group
    (c) Contribution Research Group
84. Who was invited to form a group (CRG) to undertake the work in 1952?
    (a) E.C. Richardson (b) S.R. Ranganathan
    (c) B.C. Vickery
85. When was DDC made available in machine readable form?
    (a) 1982 (b) 1984 (c) 1986
86. Who conducted DDC online project in 1985?
    (a) Library of Congress (b) Forest Press (c) CRG
87. Which catalogue inspired Dr. S.R. Ranganathan to work on value of the classified pattern?
    (a) Library of Congress Catalogue
    (b) British Museum Catalogue
    (c) Pittsburgh Classified Catalogue
88. When did Dr. S.R. Ranganathan prepare sample schedules for different facts and experimented on synthesized numbers?
    (a) March 1924 (b) March 1925
    (c) June 1924 (d) June 1925

89. When was the colon classification scheme prepared in a manuscript form made ready for the press?

(a) 1931 (b) 1932 (c) 1933 (d) 1934

90. Which book, written by Dr. S.R. Ranganathan in 1937 is called 'Gita' of colon classification scheme?

(a) *Elements of Library Classification*

(b) *Five Laws of Library Science*

(c) *Prolegomena*

(d) *Canons and Headings*

91. When was colon classification prepared and published?

(a) 1938 (b) 1939 (c) 1940 (d) 1941

92. When did Dr. S.R. Ranganathan retire from Madras University as Librarian?

(a) 1943 (b) 1944 (c) 1945 (d) 1946

93. For how much time Dr. S.R. Ranganathan remained in Benaras Hindu University Library?

(a) 1944-1947 (b) 1945-1947

(c) 1944-1946 (d) 1944-1948

94. Which international conference was attended by Dr. S.R. Ranganathan as a special invitee in September 1947?

(a) IFLA (b) FID Conference

(c) UNESCO (d) British Museum

95. Which annual conference was attended and Jubilee address given by Dr. S.R. Ranganathan in U.S.A.?

(a) LA Conference (b) ALA Jubilee Conference

(c) IFLA Conference (d) FID Conference

96. In what capacity Dr. S.R. Ranganathan attended FID/CA Committee on General Theory of Classification in 1951?

(a) Special invitee (b) Chairperson

(c) Section-Head (d) Rapporteur General

97. Which is a National Scheme of Classification in India?
    (a) Hindi Such Vargikaran by P.N. Gaur
    (b) Colon Classification
    (c) Dewey Decimal Classification
    (d) Universal Decimal Classification

98. How many fundamental categories are devised in colon classification?
    (a) Two (b) Three (c) Four (d) Five

99. Whether subject headings are used in cataloguing system of Japan?
    (a) Yes (b) No (c) Sometimes

100. Which cataloguing code is used in Japan?
    (a) Japanese Catalogue Code (b) ALA Rules
    (c) Nippon Cataloguing Rules (d) AACR

101. Which system of filing is in practice in Japanese Libraries?
    (a) Alphabetical System
    (b) Phonetic System
    (c) Nippon Shiki System (Kunree-shiki)
    (d) Dictionary arrangement

102. Which classification scheme is followed in Japan?
    (a) Dewey Decimal Classification
    (b) Colon Classification
    (c) Nippon Decimal Classification
    (d) Universal Decimal Classification

103. Which system of subject heading is used in classified catalogue code?
    (a) Sear's list of subject heading
    (b) LC subject headings
    (c) Chain procedure
    (d) British National Bibliography

104. If there comes symbol's stage, which link is used in chain procedure?
(a) Sought link (b) Unsought link
(c) False link (d) Last link

105. With which digit, the first link of the chain starts in chain procedure?
(a) Second digit (b) Last digit
(c) Symbol digit (d) First digit

106. If link ends with a chronological number of two digits, which link is used in chain procedure?
(a) Unsought link (b) Last link
(c) False link (d) Sought link

107. Which is an ideal arrangement for the entries in a classified documentation list, according to Dr. S.R. Ranganathan?
(a) Alphabetical arrangement
(b) Selected subject arrangement
(c) Everywhere Apupa-Pattern
(d) Sears' List

108. What are the prerequisites for chain procedure of Dr. S.R. Ranganathan?
(a) Book classified first and catalogued later
(b) Book catalogued first and classified letter
(c) Book catalogued first and subject indexed later

109. While applying chain procedure in dictionary catalogue which entry works to link the subjects?
(a) Subject entry (b) 'See' entry
(c) 'See-also' entry (d) Class entry

110. Who laid down the international standards for documentation in its technical committee (ISO/TC46 Documentation) in 1949?
(a) IFLA (b) FID
(c) ISO (Indian Standards Organisation) (d) ABGILA

111. What are the three processes of scientific method of Dr. S.R. Ranganathan?
   (a) Observations/Zenith/Nadir
   (b) Observation/Hypothesis/Nadir
   (c) Observation/Zenith/Testing of hypothesis
   (d) Observation/Hypothesis/Testing of hypothesis

112. Who published *Directory of Indian Scientific Periodicals* started in 1976?
   (a) ICSSR (b) INSDOC
   (c) DESIDOC

113. Who is sponsor of 'Information Science Abstract' of U.S.A.?
   (a) American Library Association
   (b) American Society of Information Science
   (c) Library of Congress

114. Which are the classes belonging to same class?
   (a) Basic classes (b) Canonical classes
   (c) Coordinate classes

115. Which book was written by Dr. S.R. Ranganathan in 1944?
   (a) *Five Laws of Library Science*
   (b) *Headings and Canons*
   (c) *Library Classification: Fundamentals and Procedures*

116. Which book was written by S.C. Bradford in 1948?
   (a) *Introduction to Documentation*
   (b) *Documentation, a Study*
   (c) *Documentation*

117. How many main classes are there in library of congress classification?
   (a) Eighteen (b) Twenty (c) Twenty-one

118. Which indicator digit is used for Time Isolates in DDC?
   (a) Zero (0) (b) Double zero (00)
   (c) Inverted comma (" ")

119. What indicator digit is used for Time Isolates in UDC?
   (a) Inverted comma (" ") (b) Zero (0)
   (c) Semicolon (;)

120. For what purpose 'Spatial Contiguity Principle' is followed in CC?
   (a) Arranging the schedule of space isolates
   (b) Arranging the schedule of time isolates
   (c) Arranging the schedule of time and space isolates

121. Which author table is devised by Cutter-Sanborn?
   (a) Two figure author table
   (b) Four figure author table
   (c) Three figures author table

122. Who devised subject classification?
   (a) H.E. Bliss (b) S.R. Ranganathan
   (c) J.D. Brown

123. By which other term (name) are the alphabetical Mnemonics known?
   (a) P-scheduled Mnemonics
   (b) Systematic Mnemonics
   (c) Verbal Mnemonics

124. Name the canon which directs that each subject should be represented by one and only one class?
   (a) Canon of synonym (b) Canon of context
   (c) Canon of relevance

125. In which digits device T, V, X and Z are postulated by S.R. Ranganathan?
   (a) Gap device (b) Emptying digits
   (c) Sector device

126. In which classification scheme Common Isolates are not used?
   (a) LC Classification Scheme
   (b) Colon Classification
   (c) Subject Classification
127. Are common isolates used in Rider's International Classification?
   (a) Yes (b) No (c) At some places
128. In which language UDC is abbreviated as CDU?
   (a) German (b) French (c) Latin
129. Who is the third personality who worked for the development of UDC alongwith Paul Otlet and Henri La Fontaine?
   (a) J.D. Brown (b) C.A. Cutter
   (c) Frits Donker Durvis
130. Which classification scheme followed Cutter's Expansive Classification Scheme for preparation of its outline?
   (a) DC (b) UDC
   (c) Both DC and UDC
131. Which subject is represented by Main Class 8 in the latest edition of UDC?
   (a) Literature (b) Psychology
   (c) Language and Linguistics
132. Which sign is used to denote agglome of non-consecutive subjects in UDC?
   (a) + (plus) (b) - (minus) (c) = (equal)
133. What is the indicator digit for space in UDC?
   (a) Square Bracket (b) Slash
   (c) Circular Bracket
134. Which new Common Isolates are added to 7th edition of CC?
   (a) Property Isolates
   (b) Common matter Isolates
   (c) Common matter property Isolates

135. Which Roman Capitals are not used for Book Number in CC?
(a) L and K (b) I and K (c) I and O

136. Which Roman smalls are not used for book number in CC?
(a) i and o (b) l and r (c) r and p

137. Which are three emptying digits postulated in 7th edition of CC?
(a) T, V, X (b) R, V, X (c) T, V, W

138. How many substantive digits are used in 7th edition of CC?
(a) 58 (b) 59 (c) 60

139. Which theory was worked out by three personalities—L. Von Bertlanffy, Ervin Laszlo, Kenneth Boulding for Universe of Knowledge?
(a) General theory (b) Group theory
(c) General Systems theory

140. Who was the first President of Classification Society of India in 1983?
(a) P.J. Kaula (b) G. Bhattacharya
(c) A. Neelameghan

141. What is the basis of formation of Cutter book number?
(a) Title (b) Subject (c) Author

142. In which classification scheme 18th edition auxiliary tables are used?
(a) UDC (b) Expensive Classification
(c) DC

143. In which classification scheme the "Floating Tables" are used?
(a) UDC (b) DC (c) LC

144. Which categories were first introduced in 2nd edition of CC?
(a) Notations (b) Mnemonics
(c) Fundamental categories

145. Who is the publisher of *Indian Press Index* who started publication in 1968?
   (a) Delhi University Library
   (b) Indian Library Association
   (c) Delhi Library Association

146. Which classification scheme is used for arrangement of entries in 'Indian Library Science Abstract'?
   (a) DC (b) CC (c) UDS

147. What is the periodicity of *Guide to Indian Periodical Literature* started in 1964?
   (a) Annual (b) Half-yearly
   (c) Quarterly

148. Who is the publisher of *Library and Information Science Abstract* published from U.K.?
   (a) British Museum, London
   (b) Library Association, U.K.
   (c) CRG, London

149. Who said regarding classification 'Nothing helps the memory so much as order and classification'?
   (a) John Stuart Blackie (b) Melvil Dewey
   (c) J.S. Mill

150. Who says 'classification made ape a man'?
   (a) E.C. Richardson (b) S.R. Ranganathan
   (c) Melvil Dewey

151. Which principle directs to 'keep like things together and unlike separately' in classification?
   (a) Principle of helpful sequence
   (b) Principle of characterstics
   (c) Principle of arrays

152. Which is the system of arrangement of books on the shelves in modern libraries?
   (a) By Author (b) By Subject
   (c) By Accession Number

153. Francis Bacon (Baconian Classification) (1561-1626) has divided universe of ideas in to which of the following groups?
   (a) History, Poetry, Philosophy
   (b) History, Geography and Science
   (c) History, Philosophy and Literature

154. Who has divided knowledge in two groups – Pure discipline and Applied discipline?
   (a) Francis Bacon (b) Thomas Hobbes
   (c) August Comte

155. Who said: 'The foundation of a library is a book, the foundation of librarianship is classification'?
   (a) W.C. Berwick Sayers (b) Melvil Dewey
   (c) H.E. Bliss

156. First use of classificatory technique is found in:
   (a) Alexandria (b) Assyrian library of surbanipal
   (c) Pergamun

157. Who introduced 'Nande system' of library classification?
   (a) Gabriel Nande (b) George Nande
   (c) Gabriel Martin

158. Brunet made his classification system as the basis of the classified part of his *Manual du Libraire et de L'Amateru des Livres* in:
   (a) 1800 (b) 1802 (c) 1804

159. Which classification was used in University of Halle, German System in 1888?
   (a) Otto Hartwig's Classification
   (b) Halle Classification
   (c) DC based 'German Classification Scheme'

160. The French Encyclopedia of 'Diderot' was based on:
   (a) Baconian System
   (b) Conrad Gesner's system
   (c) Nande system

161. What is the first name of FID?
   (a) International Institute of Bibliography
   (b) Institute of International Bibliography
   (c) International Institute of Documentation

162. Which classification code was devised by William S. Merrill in 1928?
   (a) Merrill's code of classification
   (b) Merrill's code for classifiers
   (c) Merrill's classification code

163. Who used computer in classification called Automatic Keyboard Classification in 1973?
   (a) Sparck Jones (b) CRG (c) ALA

164. Which term is given to 'any existent concrete or conceptual, that is a thing or an idea'?
   (a) Aggregate (b) Entity (c) Facet

165. A finite number of entities or known entities constitutes:
   (a) Infinite Universe (b) Finite Universe
   (c) Attributes

166. What term is given to 'any property or quality or quantitative measures of an entity'?
   (a) Aggregate (b) Attribute
   (c) Characteristics

167. The process of sorting the entities of a universe on the basis of a particular characteristics, is called:
   (a) Division or classification (b) Group of subject
   (c) Ranking of subject

168. The group containing one and only one entity is called:
   (a) Aggregate (b) Multiple group
   (c) Unitary group

169. An array of classes, admitting of extrapolation is known as:
   (a) Open array (b) Closed array
   (c) Discontinued array

170. An array of classes admitting of interpolation is called:
   (a) Closed array (b) Continuous array
   (c) Discontinuous array

171. Classes of the same order but not belonging to one and the same array are:
   (a) Immediate universe (b) Collateral classes
   (c) Collateral array

172. A sequence of classes made up of any given class and its universe is called:
   (a) Array (b) Chain (c) Division

173. A chain with a unitary class as its last link containing only one entity is known as:
   (a) Complete chain (b) Frozen chain
   (c) Primary chain

174. A chain with the original universe as its first link and a unitary class as its last link is called:
   (a) Frozen chain (b) Primary chain
   (c) Complete chain

175. The product of thinking, reflecting, imagination, etc. got by the intellect is called:
   (a) Knowledge (b) Idea (c) Thought

176. The totality of ideas consumed by humans is called:
   (a) Subject (b) Idea (c) Knowledge

177. A subject of greater extension and small intension is called:
   (a) Micro subject (b) Macro subject
   (c) Complex subject

178. A subject of small extension and greater intension is called:
   (a) Macro subject (b) Micro subject
   (c) Basic subject

179. A generic term used to denote any component, be it a basic subject or an isolate, of a compound subject is called:
   (a) Isolate (b) Facet (c) Focus

180. A classification devised to arrange books, or the library material by subject, or forms, or both, or by any recognizable logic order is called:
    (a) Knowledge classification (b) Book classification
    (c) Both

181. In which canon a characteristic used as the basis for the classification of a universe should continue unchanged?
    (a) Canon of permanence (b) Canon of relevance
    (c) Canon of ascertainability

182. In which canon the classes in an array of classes, and reranked isolates in an array of an array reranked isolates should be mutually exclusive?
    (a) Canon of exclusiveness (b) Canon of relevance
    (c) Canon of exhaustiveness

183. In which canon a chain of classes or of ranked isolates should comprise one class or one ranked isolate, as the case may be, of each and every order that lies between the order of the first link and the last link of the chain?
    (a) Canon of differentiation
    (b) Canon of exhaustiveness
    (c) Canon of modulation

184. In which sequence the classes forming an array may differ with one another as regards quantity of the entities comprehended by them?
    (a) Qualitative sequence
    (b) Quantitative sequence
    (c) In both

185. In which sequence the classes forming an array may differ as regards their degree of complexity?
    (a) Qualitative sequence
    (b) Quantitative sequence
    (c) Canon of complexity

186. In which canon the term used to denote a class or a ranked isolate in a scheme of classification should not be critical?

(a) Canon of currency

(b) Canon of enumeration

(c) Canon of reticence

187. Which value refers to the quantitative value that each digit possesses inherently? This value is generally used in counting.

(a) Ordinal value (b) Cardinal value
(c) Semantic value

188. Each digit, or digit group, used in a notational system is made to represent a particular concept, except when postulated otherwise is called:

(a) Cardinal value (b) Ordinal value
(c) Semantic value

189. Which type of notation is used as single type of notation in a scheme of classification?

(a) Mixed notation (b) Pure notation
(c) In both

190. In which canon the class number of a subject in a system of class numbers, and the isolate number of an isolate idea in a system of isolate numbers, should be unique?

(a) Canon of homonym (b) Canon of synonym
(c) Canon of currency

191. Which device is used to specify new foci by means of their dates of origin?

(a) Geographical Device

(b) Chronological Device

(c) Subject Device

192. Which of the following replaces an alphabetical subject index in conventional faceted classification and serves as an index to the classification system?

(a) Terminology (b) Thesaurus
(c) Terms

193. Who was the founder of the Journal *Library World* in 1898?

(a) J.D. Brown (b) H.E. Bliss
(c) F.B.V. Bacon (d) Ina Roberts

194. In which year 'subject classification' was compiled by J.D. Brown?

(a) 1905 (b) 1906 (c) 1907 (d) 1908

195. Which classification scheme was contributed by C.A. Cutter?

(a) Bibliographic Classification
(b) Dewey Decimal Classification
(c) Knowledge Classification
(d) Expansive Classification

196. Which post was held by Luther Harris Evans in UNESCO?

(a) Director General (b) Chairman
(c) Director (d) Secretary

197. Who was the naturalist who contributed 'Bibliotheque Universalle', first bibliographical system?

(a) J Gutenberg (b) H.E. Haines
(c) Conrad Von Gesner (d) R. Flint

198. What is the term used for 'back edge of the book on which call number is written'?

(a) Book cover (b) Spine
(c) Book plate (d) Book back

199. What term is used for 'entries on back of main card, referring to other cards relating to a book'?

(a) Title (b) Note section
(c) Tracing (d) Series note

200. Which card is a standard form of card, usually main card, which is used for all added entries?

(a) Unit card (b) Duplicate card
(c) Uniterm card (d) Main entry card

201. Which term is used for 'words describing specific subjects used in coordinate indexing?
 (a) Unit card (b) Synonyms
 (c) Uniterms (d) Visible index

202. Which classification scheme is used in British National Bibliography and Whitaker's cumulative book index (London)?
 (a) CC (b) UDC
 (c) Expensive Classification (d) DC

203. When did 'Books in Print' in U.K. start its publication in London?
 (a) 1866 (b) 1867 (c) 1868 (d) 1869

204. Which will be the place of community in Geographical area (National Group) in the schedule of 'V' HISTORY?
 (a) Matter (b) Space (c) Personality

205. What is the full form of OPAC?
 (a) Off-line Public Access Centre
 (b) On-line Public Access Catalogue
 (c) Organisation of Personal Access Catalogue
 (d) Oher Products Access Catalogue

206. When was Columbia College (now University) joined by Melvil Dewey on a salary of $ 3500 per year?
 (a) 1882 (b) 1883 (c) 1884 (c) 1855

207. Which edition of DC came out edited by Walter Stanley Biscoe, during Dewey's services in Columbia?
 (a) Edition 17-18 (b) Edition 17-19
 (c) Edition 18-19

208. At what age Melvil Dewey presented his project to develop classification before the library committee of Amherst College on May 8, 1873?
 (a) 20 years (b) 21 years
 (c) 23 years (d) 24 years

209. How many notations are assigned for main classes of DDC in 0-9 from .0000001 to .9999999?
   (a) 9 classes (b) 7 classes
   (c) 10 classes (d) 11 classes

210. Which notation is allotted for bibliography for subject bibliographies?
   (a) 0 (b) 00 (c) 000 (d) 0000

211. In which sections ten main classes are divided for further expansion of subject?
   (a) 9 divisions and 1 general division
   (b) 9 sections and 1 general section
   (c) 9 subjects and 1 general subject

212. Which is further division of 9 divisions and 1 general division of main classes?
   (a) 9 sections (b) 8 sections
   (c) 10 sections (d) 11 sections

213. Which notation is used before standard subdivisions?
   (a) 0 (b) 00 (c) None

214. Was there a separate relative index in 1st edition to 15th edition?
   (a) Yes (b) No Index
   (c) Index in the last pages of DDC edition

215. How many total entries are there in relative index of 19th edition?
   (a) 70,000 (b) 75,000
   (c) 80,000 (d) 85,000

216. In how many parts is DDC divided after 16th to 18th edition?
   (a) Schedule/Relative Index (two parts)
   (b) Schedule includes relative index (joint)
   (c) Relative index with schedule (joint)

217. Which classification scheme constructs numbers with provision of 'point of view'?
   (a) DC (b) UDC (c) CC

218. Which sequence of characteristics in CC is correct in literature?

(a) Language-Form-Author-Work
(b) Form-Author-Language-Work
(c) Work-Form-Author-Language

219. In which pattern subjects are arranged in the sequence—alien, penumbral, umbral, penumbral alien, helpful sequence? (Ranganathan)

(a) Array (b) Chain
(c) Apupa (d) Attribute

220. Which guiding principles derived from the normative principles of a subject of S.R. Ranganathan?

(a) Chain (b) Canons
(c) Cononical class

221. Which device is known as the further division of a class by digits expressing date and time?

(a) Alphabetical device (b) Chronological device
(c) Subject device

222. Which number is an ordinal number representing the position of a class in a scheme of classification? (Ranganathan)

(a) Collection number (b) Book number
(c) Class number

223. Which facet can occur in any of general classes of many main classes? (Ranganathan)

(a) Common isolate (b) Common facet
(c) Facet formula

224. What is that notation called in which the place values of the digits remain intact when an extra digit is added at the end of the term?

(a) Dependent facet (b) Diffuse facet
(c) Decimal fraction (d) Isolate

225. What do you mean by any single symbolic mark that occurs in a class term?

(a) Notation (b) Digit (c) Facet

226. What is meant if the totality of the sub-classes of a basic class is derived by the use of a single term of characteristic? (Ranganathan)

(a) Focus (b) Genus
(c) Digit (d) Facet

227. Which hospitality is known as "the quality of a notation which permits extrapolation and interpolation in an array"? (Ranganathan)

(a) Hospitality in chain (b) Hospitality in array
(c) Helpful sequence

228. Which hospitality is known "the quality of a notation to accommodate any number of sub-classes in a chain"?

(a) Hospitality in array (b) Hospitality in chain
(c) Helpful sequence

229. What term you define by "breaking down a subject into facet"?

(a) Focus (b) Facet analysis (c) Foci

230. How many principles for isolate sequence, are devised by S.R. Ranganathan?

(a) 6 (b) 7 (c) 8 (d) 9

231. Which analysis deals with the examination of possible number of zones of ideas in the structure of knowledge in arrays of different order?

(a) Sector analysis (b) Zone analysis
(c) Facet analysis

232. How many classification schemes are applied in Indian National Bibliography?

(a) Colon Classification
(b) Dewey Decimal Classification
(c) Universal Decimal Classification
(d) Colon Classification and Dewey Decimal Classification

233. Binary system of number uses only:

(a) Two digits (b) Four digits
(c) Eight digits (d) Six digits

234. Canon of characteristics are parts of:
(a) Verbal plane (b) Notational plane
(c) Idea plane (d) Structural plane

INFORMATION SCIENCE & DOCUMENTATION

235. When did microfilm first come into prominence during the France-Prussian War?
(a) 1865 (b) 1870 (c) 1872

236. Who first photographed an abbreviated version of the document on a tiny film measuring 30 × 55mm and inserted into a small tube in Nov. 1870?
(a) Rene Dagron (b) James Lowee
(c) Ronald Ellee

237. Microfilm, in its infancy, involved which three R's?
(a) Reduction, Retrieval and Reproduction
(b) Reporting, Reduction and Reproduction
(c) Recalling, Retrieval and Reproduction

238. Which is a trade name for an Opaque Card 6″ × 9″ containing normally 100 micro-images in rows printed by photo lithography?
(a) Microfiche (b) Micro-card
(c) Micro-print

239. What is the trade name for the Opaque Card approximately 5″ × 3″ containing micro-images in rows?
(a) Microfiche (b) Microlex (c) Micro-card

240. What is a trade name for an Opaque Card 6″ × 8″ containing 200 micro-images?
(a) Micro-card (b) Microprint
(c) Microlex

241. Which camera is used for larger documents such as engineering drawings or thicker documents such as books, in microfilming?
(a) Flow type camera (b) Planetary type camera
(c) Roll-film camera

242. What is the largest roll film size used in microfilm?
   (a) 75mm and 150mm width
   (b) 90mm and 110mm width
   (c) 75mm and 120mm width

243. Which size of film is used to photograph a large area of material contained in separate items and to photograph a number of separate pages by one exposure?
   (a) 35mm (b) 75mm (c) 105mm

244. Which format of microfiche was adopted by British Standard Institution?
   (a) 105 × 148mm and 75 × 125mm
   (b) 75 × 105mm and 105 × 125mm
   (c) None of the above

245. Who introduced microprint card?
   (a) Albert Jelley (b) Albert Bone
   (c) Fremont Rider

246. What is appropriate size of microlex containing two hundred pages on each size of card?
   (a) 5½ × 7½" (b) 6½ × 8½" (c) 7 × 9"

247. When was the technique for microfilm by coating a transparent material with a diazo compound and coupler first developed by Kalle organisation?
   (a) 1925 (b) 1930 (c) 1932

248. Which photographic film was developed by Kalvar Corporation in America which requires neither chemicals nor darkroom and can be developed by heat?
   (a) Diazo (b) Kalvar (c) Rolex

249. Which indexing system uses a single term and an accessories number of document as an indicator of reference?
   (a) NEPHIS (b) Relative Index
   (c) KWIC (d) PRECIS

250. 'Universal Bibliographical Control' is a programme of:
   (a) FID (b) IFLA (c) UNISIST (d) ALA

251. Delphi technique is related to:
(a) Budgeting (b) Statistics
(c) Forecasting (d) Performance Evaluation

252. The unit card principle is associated with:
(a) Sheaf catalogue (b) Card catalogue
(c) Printed catalogue
(d) Machine readable catalogue

253. 'National Index of Translations' is published by:
(a) NASSADOC (b) DESIDOC
(c) SENDOC (d) INSDOC

254. An abstract which is written for a specific group of users is known as:
(a) Critical abstract (b) Slanted abstract
(c) Author abstract (d) Indicative abstract

255. Which of the following is considered as the most important component in research design?
(a) Observation (b) Formation of hypothesis
(c) Case study (d) Review of literature

256. 'NICDROM' is a sectoral information centre relating to:
(a) Drug research (b) Organisation management
(c) CD-ROM (d) Bibliometrics

257. What was the name of the Imperial Library of Calcutta in 1948?
(a) Central Reference Library
(b) Secretariat Library
(c) Asiatic Library
(d) National Library of India

258. Which one of the following is an example of an operating system?
(a) DOS (b) Word Star
(c) dBase (d) LOTUS 1-2-3

259. 'Indian Science Abstract' is brought out by:
(a) DESIDOC (b) INSA
(c) INSDOC (d) NISSAT

260. *Books in Print* is a:
   (a) National Bibliography
   (b) Trade Bibliography
   (c) Retrospective Bibliography
   (d) Subject Bibliography

261. The first commercial Online system to be introduced was:
   (a) DIALOG (b) BRS (c) ORBIT (d) OCLC

262. What is an interview?
   (a) A total of research
   (b) A process of research
   (c) A type of research
   (d) A method of presentation of data

263. POPSI, PRECIS, Chain Procedure and SLIC are examples of:
   (a) Indexing System (b) Classification System
   (c) Cataloguing Codes (d) Abstracting Procedure

264. Indicate the name of philosopher who was the exponent of scientific method:
   (a) Aristotle (b) Bacon
   (c) Confucious (d) Descartes

265. The concept of 'Technological gatekeepers' was first propounded by:
   (a) Allen (b) Diana Crane
   (c) De Solla Price (d) Derek Austin

266. Library Legislation supports the Public Library Movement by:
   (a) Ensuring that funds are made available
   (b) Establishing local library authority
   (c) Making library service free
   (d) All the above

267. The extension service to the blinds by a public library is justified by:
   (a) The fourth law of library science
   (b) The fifth law of library science
   (c) The second law of library science
   (d) All the laws of library science

268. If you are asked to arrange the concepts of information and data in ascending order of complexity, which of the following is correct?
   (a) Data-information-knowledge
   (b) Knowledge-information-data
   (c) Information-data-knowledge
   (d) Information-knowledge-data

269. JOCLAI includes:
   (a) ILA and IASLIC
   (b) IASLIC, GILA and ILA
   (c) ILA, IASLIC and IATLIS
   (d) All the State Library Associations

270. IATLIS is an organisation of:
   (a) Academic Libraries
   (b) Teachers of Library and Information Science
   (c) Special Libraries
   (d) School Libraries

271. *World of Learning* is a:
   (a) Journal
   (b) Directory
   (c) Textbook on education
   (d) Bibliography on education

272. In which conference subject entries were recommended for the first time?
   (a) Calcutta Conference, 1964
   (b) ALA Conference, 1967
   (c) IFLA Conference, 1959
   (d) Paris Conference, 1961

273. Which of the following is not a secondary source of information?

(a) An abstracting journal (b) A handbook
(c) A statistical digest (d) A patent

274. Which of the following is a Union catalogue?

(a) Ulritch's International Periodical Directory
(b) New serials titles
(c) Press in India
(d) NUCSSI

275. Entries in Indian Science Abstracts are arranged according to:

(a) DDC (b) UDC (c) LC (d) CC

276. Directing user to the right source of information is called:

(a) Current awareness service (b) Digest service
(c) Data service (d) Referral service

277. Intellectual Property Rights are recognized as:

(a) Copyright (b) Patent
(c) Neither (A) nor (B) (d) Both (A) and (B)

278. 'Gazette' gives information about:

(a) Place to see
(b) History of places
(c) Old records
(d) Official announcements & notifications

279. Which of the following can be considered as a key attribute in a bibliographic database?

(a) ISBN (b) Author
(c) Title (d) Main entry access point

280. 'International Conference on Cataloguing Principles' (Paris) was held in the year:

(a) 1969 (b) 1961 (c) 1967 (d) 1972

281. 'Wall-Picture principle' is one of the principles of:

(a) Helpful sequence (b) Alphabetical sequence
(c) Facet sequence (d) Canonical sequence

282. In retrieval system the coordination of concepts done by the searches' search stage is known as:
(a) Pre-coordinate (b) Post-coordinate
(c) Under coordinate (d) Over coordinate

283. Measurement of performance of a service/activity in relation to cost is:
(a) Cost effectiveness (b) Cost Accounting
(c) Cost analysis (d) Performance analysis

284. Shelf list cards:
(a) Help the arrangement of shelves
(b) Are used in stock verification
(c) Represent each volume on the shelf
(d) All of the above

285. The method of budgeting which is not concerned with what happened previously but is more concerned with the requirement of the future is known as:
(a) One budget (b) Programme budget
(c) Formula budget (d) Zero-based budget

286. The concept of self-renewal was introduced by:
(a) Atkinson (b) Dr. Parry
(c) Danton (d) M.B. Line

287. Good Office Committee (GOC), New Delhi helps in determining:
(a) Foreign exchange rates
(b) Names of foreign agents & vendors
(c) Books available in the market
(d) Which books to buy

288. Research of Elton Mayo at the Western Electric Hawthorn plant revealed that:
(a) Workers are more motivated by social rewards
(b) Workers are more motivated by economic incentives
(c) Both (a) and (b)
(d) Neither (a) nor (b)

289. Which of the following networks is not primarily for academic purpose?
(a) ERNET (b) NICNET
(c) JANET (d) INFLIBNET

290. UNISIST is a joint programme of:
(a) UNESCO and FID (b) UNESCO & IFLA
(c) UNESCO and IFM (d) UNESCO & ICSU

291. Among the following which is not a NISSAT sectorial centre?
(a) National Chemical Laboratory
(b) National Informatics Centre
(c) Central Drug Research Institute
(d) ATIRA

292. 'OPAC' stands for:
(a) Ohio Province Acquisition Consortium
(b) Online public access catalogue
(c) Ohio public and academic library centre
(d) None of above

293. Which is Indian input centre for AGRIS:
(a) ICAR (b) The Ministry of Agriculture
(c) IARI (d) None of the above

294. Which of the following languages is not a computer programming language?
(a) Fortran (b) Basic (c) Cobol (d) Asc II

295. Computer terminology 'C' refers to:
(a) Console (b) CPU
(c) Memory (d) Programming language

296. Integrated circuits were used in:
(a) First generation computers
(b) Second generation computers
(c) Third generation computers
(d) All the above

297. Arrange the following storage device according to increasing capacity: (a) magnetic tape (b) CD-ROM (c) Floppy Disk (c) Magnetic Disk:
   (a) c a d b
   (b) a b c d
   (c) d c a b
   (d) d a b c

298. Electronic Mail is delivered through:
   (a) Postman
   (b) Counter
   (c) Speed Post
   (d) Computer & Modem

299. In an empirical study of the effect of open access on borrowing patterns: open access is:
   (a) An independent variable
   (b) A dependent variable
   (c) Not a variable at all
   (d) An intervening variable

300. The four cell design is used in:
   (a) Surveys
   (b) Experiments
   (c) Case studies
   (d) Historical research

301. In search on motivation among university library personal, if the researcher takes every fifth person from category of staff, e.g. Jr.Librarian, Asstt. Librarian, Dy. Librarian, etc. it would be:
   (a) A random sample
   (b) A stratified sample
   (c) The whole population
   (d) Not a representative sample

302. Hypothesis is a:
   (a) Generalisation
   (b) Law
   (c) Theory
   (d) Theory of the tested

303. Who developed PLEXUS, a prototype reference export system in the University of London?
   (a) Helen Books and Alina Vickery
   (b) Connie Dowell and Crews
   (c) Susan Humphrey and Nancy E. Miller

304. In which language the PLEXUS software is written?
  (a) Pascal (b) Cobol (c) Fortran

305. Which network covers the Colleges and Universities in India?
  (a) DELNET (b) INFLIBNET
  (c) BONET (d) CALNET

306. CAB, AGRIS, AGRICOLA CD-ROM database covers the subject:
  (a) Agriculture (b) Maths (c) Sociology

307. What is store capacity in 12cm diameter CD-ROM disk?
  (a) 230,000 records (b) 270,000 records
  (c) 350,000 records

308. What is the normal size of microfiche?
  (a) 14cm × 9cm (b) 14.5cm × 10.5cm
  (c) 14.5cm × 10cm

309. A standard microfiche can accommodate:
  (a) 75 pages (b) 98 pages (c) 105 pages

310. Closest microform to fiche in terms of format is:
  (a) Pocket microfilm (b) Tab microfilm
  (c) Jacket microfilm

311. Who inaugurated Library Research Circle in Bangalore in 1958?
  (a) C.G. Vishwanathan (b) P.N. Kaula
  (c) S.R. Ranganathan

312. Who planned SIRNET as a computer communication network for exchange of information among its 40 odd laboratories and R&D institutions?
  (a) ICAR (b) INSDOC (c) CSIR

313. The organisation of Indigenous Online database services of food technology was helped by:
  (a) INFLIBNET (b) NICNET
  (c) INDONET (d) SIRNET

314. Online database services of leather technology, natural products, radio physics and medicine plants were supported by:

(a) INDONET (b) SIRNET (c) ERNET

315. Which network is planned as a four-layer system consisting of?

(a) Backbone nodes (b) City nodes
(c) Laboratory nodes (d) All the above

316. SIRNET plays an important role in resource sharing with the services of:

(a) Electronic mail (b) INTERNET
(c) EARN

317. INSDOC produced indigenous databases:

(a) Current contents of Indian Journals

(b) Polymer Science Database

(c) National Union Catalogue of Scientific Services in India

(d) All the above

318. SIRNET has at present only:

(a) One mail node located at INSDOC

(b) Two mail node located at CDRI

(c) None of them

319. ERNET is connected with:

(a) UUNET (Unix User Network) (b) INTERNET
(c) SIRNET

320. Which is International Network?

(a) SIRNET (b) JANET (c) VIDYANET

321. INSDOC has established access to over 1800 International databases through VSNL-GPSS facility on:

(a) 10 different hosts (b) 12 different hosts
(c) 15 different hosts

322. Department of Communication, Govt. of India set up:

(a) SIRNET (b) I-NET (c) VIDYANET

323. NICNET was established by:
   (a) NIC, New Delhi (b) INFLIBNET, Ahmedabad
   (c) CSIR, New Delhi

324. NIC established ICMRNIC in collaboration with:
   (a) CDRI (b) ICMR (c) INSDOC

325. CMC Ltd. developed INDONET in:
   (a) 1984 (b) 1985 (c) 1986

326. INDONET provides many services including:
   (a) Translation service
   (b) Reprographic Application
   (c) Bibliographic Application

327. Vikram is Packet Switched Public Data Network with network management centre at:
   (a) Nagpur (b) Bangalore (c) Delhi

328. Professor V.K.R.V. Rao, member of Planning Commission, Incharge of Education was the Chairman of the Committee in 1969 who recommended the setting up of:
   (a) INSDOC (b) ICSSR (c) NASSADOC

329. ICSSR has established the regional centres in:
   (a) Mumbai, Hyderabad, Kolkata, Shillong, New Delhi, Chandigarh
   (b) Mumbai, Secunderabad, Kolkata, Gauwahati, New Delhi, Shimla
   (c) Mumbai, Hyderabad, Patna, Shillong, New Delhi, Shimla

330. ICSSR established Inter Library Resource Centre (ILRC) in 1973 jointly with:
   (a) Delhi University (b) Jamia Millia (c) JNU

331. The Planning Commission appointed a working group on modernization of library services and information for:
   (a) Eighth Five-Year Plan (b) Seventh Five-Year Plan
   (c) Ninth Five-Year Plan

332. SNDT, Mumbai has developed:
    (a) Data Archives of ICSSR
    (b) Database of periodical database and issue SUCHIKA
    (c) SUCHAK Database

333. Information source, encoder, message, communication channel, noise, decoder and receiver/destination are the basic elements of:
    (a) Translation process (b) Bibliographic process
    (c) Communication process

334. Communication technology has two basic components:
    (a) Transmission / Encoder technology
    (b) Message / Receiver technology
    (c) Transmission / Network technology

335. The network consists of points called:
    (a) Nodes (b) Arcs (c) The topic

336. The relationship between 'nodes' of a network is described by:
    (a) Subject domain (b) Arcs
    (c) Inference engine

337. Who has categorized the languages as COBOL, PL/I; JOVIAL, PL/I; ALGOL, BASI, FORTRAN; and LISP, SNOBO?
    (a) Rammurty (b) C.R. Hildreh (c) Gilbert

338. Which of these are international networks?
    (a) INFLIBNET (b) CALIBNET (c) INSPEC

339. Which network is set up by Deptt. of Biotechnology, Govt. of India?
    (a) SIRNET (b) ERNET (c) BLISNET

340. Which of the following is a business network?
    (a) CALIBNET (b) NICNET (c) TOURNET

341. Which is a subject network?
    (a) INFLIBNET (b) COALNET (c) BONET

342. There are four different phases out of which three are section, notification, feedback. Which is the fourth?

(a) Motivation (b) Revision (c) Modification

343. What is alternative name by which manipulative index is commonly known?

(a) Pre-coordinate index (b) Post coordinate index
(c) Online index

344. Which term was coined by Mikhailov, Chernyi and Gilyarevaski?

(a) Bibliometric (b) Informatic (c) Systematic

345. What is new term of 'Bibliomatrics' coined by Alan Pritchard?

(a) Selective Bibliography
(b) Analytical Bibliography
(c) Statistical Bibliography

346. Who launched the programme of National Information System? (NITIS)?

(a) UNICEF (b) IFLA (c) UNESCO

347. What is full form of LUCI?

(a) Legal unit-based cyclic index
(b) Logical unit-based cyclic index
(c) Level unit-based circle index

348. Of which system is ACAR a National input centre?

(a) Agro-com system (b) Agro-net system
(c) AGRIS system

349. Which indexing system was devised by J.R. Sharp?

(a) SLOP indexing (b) PRECIS indexing
(c) SLIC indexing

350. In which year was the National Sample Survey Organisation (NSSO) set up?

(a) 1969 (b) 1970 (c) 1971

351. What is full form of KWIC?
 (a) Key Wave in Context
 (b) Key Word in Contact
 (c) Key Work in Context

352. Which organisation is maintaining the Common Wealth Index of unpublished transactions?
 (a) UNESCO (b) FID (c) ASLIB

353. Who is publishing NIT (National Index of Translation) in India?
 (a) ICSSR
 (b) Indian Science Institute, Bangalore
 (c) INSDOC

354. Who coined the term 'Information Retrieval' in 1950?
 (a) E.C. Richardson (b) M.E. Coole
 (c) Colvin Mooers

355. Who introduced the concept of Selective Dissemination of Information (SDI) in 1958?
 (a) H. Peter Luhn (b) Peter Luhn
 (c) McColvin

356. When was the NISSAT established?
 (a) May 1976 (b) May 1977 (c) May 1978

357. How many members IFLA enrolled in 1994 in 30 countries?
 (a) 1272 (b) 1281 (c) 1265

358. Who introduced core programme in General Conference of Nairobi, Kenya?
 (a) FID (b) IFLA (c) UNESCO

359. In which year IFLA introduced ALP core programme?
 (a) 1982 (b) 1984 (c) 1985

360. In which year was the Regional Standing Committee for Asia organised by IFLA?
 (a) 1980 (b) 1989 (c) 1990

361. What is the year of establishment of Dhaka University of Bangladesh?

(a) 1921 (b) 1923 (c) 1925

362. When was BANSDOC(Bangladesh National Scientific & Technical Documentation Centre) established?

(a) 1972 (b) 1973 (c) 1974

363. Who was the Chairman of Central Committee of UNESCO & ICSU in 1967?

(a) F.A. Siviridov (b) D.J. Foskett

(c) I. Dahlberg (d) A. Vandar Loan

364. In which year was FID Conference held in Budapest?

(a) 1972 (b) 1973 (c) 1974

365. Which was the first Indian Education Commission appointed by British India Govt. in 1882?

(a) East India Education Commission

(b) Indian Education Commission

(c) Hunter Commission

366. Who was the Governor General who appointed Indian University Commission in 1902?

(a) Lord Lansdown (b) Lord Curzon

(c) Lord Hunter

367. Who was the Chairman of Calcutta University Commission in 1917 who suggested for an effective university library?

(a) Sir Michael Sadlar (b) Sir William Moore

(c) Sir Armered George

368. When was first analog computer installed at ISI, Calcutta?

(a) 1947-1957 (b) 1948-1955

(c) 1947-1959

369. When did Deptt. of Electronics come into existence?

(a) 1969 (b) 1970 (c) 1971

370. When did Online catalogue OPAC appear?

(a) 1981 (b) 1982 (c) 1980

371. Are video disks digitally coded information?
(a) Yes (b) No

372. Teletex is also known as:
(a) Broadcast videotext (b) Interactive videotext

373. View data are also known as:
(a) Hypertext (b) Interactive videotext

374. Who used hypertext term for the first time?
(a) Vannevar Bush (b) Douglas C. Eugelbart
(c) C.K. Ramaiah

375. Hypertext system is known as:
(a) Online system (b) No line system
(c) HM system

376. Which are E-mail options?
(a) Telex based, teletex based, facsimile based and computer based
(b) Super telex, teletex, videotext, telex based

377. Who developed software 'DOOT' computer software package?
(a) NCST (b) NIC (c) ERNET group

378. Which communication software was developed by ERNET group?
(a) X-300 (b) X-500 (c) X-400

379. Who developed INDNET in 1986, the first computer network?
(a) CMC Ltd. (b) NIC
(c) BTS Programme

380. How many Regional Centres have been established by ICSSR in India?
(a) Five (b) Six (c) Four (d) Seven

381. Which network was launched in collaboration of India and UNESCO in 1986?
(a) APINESS (b) WINAP (c) DELNET

382. When was the satellite first used for communication?

(a) 1960 (b) 1961 (c) 1962

383. Who launched TELESTAR in 1962?

(a) AT&T (b) NIC (c) NASA

384. Who established CD-ROM at National Aerospace Laboratory, Bangalore in 1988?

(a) NIC (b) NISSAT (c) DESIDOC

385. Who was the Chairman of the Committee for Library Development appointed by the Bombay Government in 1939?

(a) S.A. Farooqui (b) M.S. Farlane
(c) A.A.A. Fyzee

386. At which place was ILA conference held in 1988?

(a) Tiruchirapalli (b) Madras
(c) Bangalore

387. When was CD-ROM introduced in library and information science?

(a) Jan. 1985 (b) Jan. 1986
(c) Jan. 1987

388. Who introduced CD-PAC for the first time in 1985?

(a) Brodart (b) Karch (c) Miller

389. Which is famous CD-ROM on Indian people, culture, land and history of India set by the Compact Disk India Ltd.?

(a) Krishna (b) Karishma
(c) Indian Culture

390. Can digital optical video disks store computer processible, character coded-data, or digitized document images?

(a) Yes (b) No

391. When did satellite technology start in use for international video and voice transmission?

(a) 1955 (b) 1960 (c) 1965

392. When did India launch the 44 metre polar satellite launch vehicle-PSLV, 922 kg remote sensing satellite?
    (a) Jan. 5, 1996 (b) Feb. 14, 1996
    (c) March 21, 1996

393. Do you agree that videotex (t) services combine video and database technologies to disseminate combinations of computer generated textual and graphic information to modified television receivers or other relatively inexpensive terminals?
    (a) Yes (b) No

394. Which are two broad groups of videotext system?
    (a) Teletext/view data (b) Broadcast videotext
    (c) Teletext/hypertext

395. What is other term used for view data?
    (a) Hypertext (b) Interactive videotext
    (c) Broadcast videotext

396. Who conceived the 'hypertext' for the first time in 1945 which was known as 'Memax'?
    (a) Vennevar Bush (b) C.K. Ramaiah
    (c) While Zink

397. Which is the first E-mail network company in India licensed by Deptt. of Telecommunication?
    (a) ICNET Ltd. (b) MTNL (c) ERNET

398. Which is the first voice-mail technology introduced in India?
    (a) MTNL (b) ICNET (c) DTMF

399. When was 'Hybrid mail technology' first introduced in India?
    (a) Jan. 1, 1995 (b) Jan. 5, 1995
    (c) Jan. 14, 1995

400. Does 'Hybrid mail service' use a combination of computers and VSAT?
    (a) Yes (b) No

401. When was Integrated Services Digital Network (ISDN) introduced through Hi-tech imported exchange set up in 6 cities—Delhi, Bombay, Calcutta, Madras, Bangalore and Ahmedabad?

(a) Oct. 11, 1995 (b) Oct. 17, 1995
(c) Oct. 23, 1995

402. When was Cellular Mobile Phone system (Pocket telephone) introduced in India?

(a) 1991 (b) 1993 (c) 1995

403. In which phone technology SIM card is used?

(a) Telephone service (b) Cellphone service
(c) Radio page service

404. Do you agree that 'Radio Paging Technology' is a one-way communication service to alert a person who cannot be contacted over telephone?

(a) Yes (b) No

405. Which paging service is available over FM Network in Delhi within a radius of 50 Kms?

(a) Cellphone service (b) Radio paging service
(c) NIC service

406. In which year Library of Congress developed the mark format for bibliographical data on magnetic tape?

(a) 1956 (b) 1960 (c) 1962

407. What was the first hypertext system named in 1960?

(a) NO LINE SYSTEM (NLS) (b) AUGMENT
(c) FRESS

408. What does the term 'hyper' of Hypertext refer to?

(a) Over or in excess (b) More or increased
(c) Expands or spread

409. Who used the term 'cyberspace' for the first time?

(a) William Gibson (b) Richard H. Veith
(c) William Saffady

410. What is full form of WWW?
   (a) Word Wide Web (b) Whole World Web
   (c) World Wide Web
411. What is full form of 'Internet'?
   (a) Internet complete system
   (b) Internet computer system
   (c) Internet work system
412. When did IRNET project start in India?
   (a) 1985 (b) 1986 (c) 1987
413. What is standard B.S. number of an Index?
   (a) B.S. 3650 : 1953 (b) B.S. 3675 : 1954
   (c) B.S. 3700 : 1954
414. What is library catalogue?
   (a) Limited to one or more libraries
   (b) Not limited to one or more libraries
   (c) Neither (a) nor (b)
415. Which index was recognized as good index during the seventeenth century?
   (a) Index of History of Great Britannia (1611)
   (b) Index of Acts and Ordinances of Parliament (1656)
   (c) Neither (a) nor (b)
416. In which year *Encyclopedia Britannica* published separate volume of index?
   (a) 1870 (b) 1872 (c) 1874
417. Who brought out the index to Periodical literature, 1801-1906?
   (a) Dr. Johnson (b) Scobell
   (c) William Frederick Poole
418. In which country the index society was formed in 1877?
   (a) U.S.A. (b) U.K. (c) India

419. What are three approaches of Indexes?
   (a) Subject, Author, Document approach
   (b) Author, Title and Series approach
   (c) Subject, Document and Series approach

420. Which index is termed, if there is systematic list of cited and citing documents?
   (a) Subject index (b) Author index
   (c) Citation index

421. Which is the index in which the coordination of components is done at the input level?
   (a) Post-coordinate index
   (b) Pre-coordinate index
   (c) Permuterm subject index

422. Which is the index in which the coordination is effected at the output stage?
   (a) Pre-coordinate index
   (b) Post-coordinate index
   (c) Cumulative index

423. For which rules catalogue was introduced by Cutter in 1876?
   (a) Rules for classified catalogue
   (b) Rules for dictionary catalogue
   (c) Rules for subject catalogue

424. In which catalogue of J. Kaiser the theoretical basis was laid down for fixing the order of significance among various components of a composite heading?
   (a) Subject indexing (b) Systematic indexing
   (c) Citation index

425. What is the order of significance among various components of a compound subject?
   (a) Thing, material and action
   (b) Thing, action, document
   (c) Thing, document energy

426. Who developed nested phrase indexing system (NEPHIS)?
(a) Timothy C. Craven (b) J. Kaiser
(c) C.A. Cutter

427. In which year A.L. Mudaliar Commission on Secondary Education submitted its report?
(a) 1950 (b) 1051 (c) 1952

428. When did PRECIS come into being?
(a) 1965 (b) 1967 (c) 1952

429. When did BNB introduce PRECIS?
(a) 1970 (b) 1971 (c) 1972

430. Which post-coordinate indexing system is based on term entry principle and introduced by Mortimer Tanbe in 1953?
(a) Uniterm indexing system (b) POPSI
(c) PRECIS

431. Who introduced keyword in title in 1856?
(a) Hans Luhn (b) Andrea Crestadoro
(c) A.C. Foskett

432. In which country did the citation index originate?
(a) India (b) U.S.A. (c) U.K.

433. Who made first effort and applied the technique of citation index in 1873?
(a) Frank Shopard (b) B.B. Lane
(c) J.D. Black

434. When was the Genetics Citation Index being brought out first?
(a) 1960 (b) 1961 (c) 1963

435. What is the periodicity of *Biography Index* being published by H.W. Wilson since 1946?
(a) Weekly (b) Quarterly (c) Fortnightly

436. Which is the first generation of OPAC?
(a) Keyword searching
(b) Improved Subject searching
(c) Machine Readable form

437. Which group is required for OPAC System?
   (a) Server, Desktop, Network
   (b) Server, Keyword, Network
   (c) Desktop, Keyword, Network

438. What is full form of HTML?
   (a) Hypertext make-up language?
   (b) Hi-Tech mark-up language
   (c) Hypertext mark-up language

439. Which OPAC System is also known as 'Web Cats'?
   (a) OPAC (b) Web OPAC (c) HTML

440. At which place was the International Conference on the improvement of Bibliographical services held in Nov. 1950?
   (a) London (b) New York (c) Paris

441. In which year was 'UNESCO Workshop on Thesaurus Construction' by means of computers held?
   (a) Nov. 1981 (b) Nov. 1983 (c) Nov. 1985

442. In which year was 'UNESCO Workshop on Information Processing Tools' held in Grazi Austria?
   (a) 1981 (b) 1983 (c) 1984

443. When was 'Panama Seminar on Education Documentation and Information' held?
   (a) 1969 (b) 1970 (c) 1971

444. Where was UNESCO's symposiums on National Libraries in Europe held in Sept. 1958?
   (a) Vienna (Austria) (b) Moscow (c) Hague

445. In which year was the FID General Assembly held in Montreal?
   (a) 1984 (b) 1985 (c) 1986

446. Who published 'The International Forum on Information and Documentation' (FID)?
   (a) IFLA (b) CFID (c) UNESCO

447. Who acquired CDS/ISIS from UNESCO?
(a) NISSAT (b) NIC (c) INFLIBNET

448. Which software has been developed by DESIDOC?
(a) SANJAY (b) TRISHNA (c) SUPERDOC

449. Who devised formula *f=eia* for optimum size of collection for public libraries?
(a) N. Stoljorov (b) Nick, Maore
(c) J.H. Shera

450. The term "Exponential growth" referrs to:
(a) Linear growth
(b) Geometrical progression
(c) Arithmetical progression
(d) Normal frequency distribution

451. A hypothesis that is tested for its rejection is:
(a) Alternative hypothesis (b) Statistical inference
(c) Observation (d) Null hypothesis

452. The three broad categories of biographical dictionaries are:
(a) General, National, Special
(b) International, National, Local
(c) General, Special, Local
(d) General, National, and International

453. The type of international networks accessible to online vendor are such as:
(a) WAN (b) MAN
(c) LAN (d) None of the above

454. Who identified pseudo abstract?
(a) T.E.R. Singer (b) C.L. Bernier
(c) A.L. Mikhaltov

455. Are preferred terms of a thesaurus known as descriptors?
(a) Yes (b) No

456. Who drafted guidelines for the establishment and development of monolingual thesauri in 1973?

(a) UNESCO (b) IFLA (c) UNISIST

457. Is INIS a decentralized non-commercial information network of 87 countries?

(a) Yes (b) No

458. With the help of which INIS are Magnetic tapes prepared?

(a) Flexowriter (b) Computer
(c) MEDLAR

459. What is periodicity of INIS Atomindex journal?

(a) Monthly (b) Quarterly
(c) Semi-monthly

460. How many items have been included in INIS database during the past 23 years?

(a) 9 lakhs items (b) 8,80,000 items
(c) 800,000 items

461. How many INIS documents are known as INIS reference series?

(a) 20 (b) 21 (c) 25

462. Who is the publisher of *Indian National Agricultural Bibliography* (INAB) published four volumes?

(a) ARIC (b) INSDOC (c) AGRIS

463. What is full form of CATV.

(a) Central Automatic Television
(b) Cable TV
(c) Communicative TV

464. When was APPLE was orbited in India?

(a) 1978 (b) 1981
(c) 1882 (d) 1985

465. Which series of the following class numbers belongs to first, second and third summaries of DDC respectively?

(a) 110, 345, 000 (b) 300, 624, 310
(c) 560, 400, 120 (d) 800, 320, 624

466. *Biography of Bibliographies* comes under the category:
(a) Primary sources (b) Secondary sources
(c) Tertiary sources (d) None of the above

467. The BARC is identified as national input centre for:
(a) AGRIS (b) INIS
(c) DEVSIS (d) SPINES

468. The device that converts digital to analog and analog to digital signals is known as:
(a) Analog computers (b) Modem
(c) VDU (d) Electrofax

469. The secondary sources of information are comprised of:
(a) Textbooks and research monographs
(b) Subject periodicals and encyclopedias
(c) Indexing and abstracting periodicals
(d) Bibliography and patents

470. What term is given to applying statistical distributions to library organisations and services?
(a) Bibliometrics (b) Informatics
(c) Librametry

471. What term is given to the application of statistical distributions to Bibliographical organisation and services?
(a) Bibliometrics (b) Librametry
(c) Informatics

472. Who used Bibliometric term for the first time in 1969?
(a) A. Pritchand (b) A. Neelameghan
(c) S.R. Ranganathan

473. A citation index is an ordered list of cited articles each of which is accompanied by a list of:
(a) Citing articles (b) Citing books
(c) Citing monographs

474. Frank Shepard developed Shepard's citations in:
(a) 1870 (b) 1871
(c) 1873

475. The Welch project of medical literature in John Hopkins Welch Medical Library of 1950 was concerned with:
(a) Abstracting (b) Indexing (citation)
(c) None of them

476. Cumulative index of the journal of the American Statistical Association published in 1959 and Cumulative Index of Annals of Mathematical Statistics published in 1962 were concerned with:
(a) Citation Indexing (b) Abstracting
(c) None of them

477. Science Citation Index is a brainchild of:
(a) Garfield (b) Shepard (c) Welch

478. Frequency of *Science Citation Index* is:
(a) Weekly (b) Monthly (c) Quarterly

479. The part citation index of *Science Citation Index* of cited authors is arranged:
(a) Alphabetically (b) Chronologically
(c) Subjectwise

480. The Source Index is an alphabetical list of:
(a) Cited authors (b) Citing authors
(c) None of the them

RESEARCH METHODS AND APTITUDE

481. In the selection of the topic of research the most important is:
(a) Value judgment (b) Project
(c) Availability of more resources

482. Which is a conjectural statement of the relation between two or more variables in a research?
(a) Hypothesis (b) Research problem
(c) Existing literature

483. Which of the following can carry clear implications for testing the stated relations in research?
(a) Research topic (b) Hypothesis
(c) Manageable size of the problem

484. Concept may be grouped into two classes:
   (a) Postulation and intuition
   (b) Postulation and behaviour
   (c) Intuition and experience

485. How many essential steps in research process are suggested by Mr. Schuller?
   (a) Ten (b) Twelve
   (c) Fifteen

486. Effectiveness of enterprise is one variable in experimental design, which is:
   (a) Dependent variable (b) Independent variable
   (c) Neither of them

487. In which class of research the independent variable is an experimental design?
   (a) Ex post-facto research (b) Post-facto research
   (c) Laboratory research

488. Laboratory experiments, field experiments, field studies and survey research are four major categories of:
   (a) Laboratory experiments (b) Project study
   (c) Neither of them

489. The Britishers used the term Operational research, while American used the term:
   (a) Operations research (b) Placement research
   (c) Applied research

490. Which is final stage of the research?
   (a) Report writing (b) Collection of data
   (c) Preparing for statistical data

491. Questionnaires and schedules are important tools of:
   (a) Scientific research (b) Operational research
   (c) Social Science research

492. Vague and ambiguous questions (in a questionnaire) should be:
   (a) Considered (b) Avoided (c) Rejected

493. Loaded questions of a questionnaire should be:
(a) Detected carefully (b) Rejected
(c) Avoided

494. Questions encouraging guess work of a questionnaire are:
(a) Dangerous (b) Favourable
(c) Not considered

495. Mail questionnaires may be used among:
(a) Literates (b) Illiterates
(c) Neither (a) nor (b)

496. Which is a device of securing answers to the questions in a form which a respondent himself fills in?
(a) Questionnaire (b) Interview
(c) Observations

497. In which basic theory of the interview, the same set of estimate should be administered equally to all respondents in the sample?
(a) Structured schedule
(b) Non-structured schedule
(c) Neither of them

498. 'A systematic and deliberate study through the eyes of spontaneous occurrences at the time they occur' is called:
(a) Observation (b) Interviewed (c) Survey

499. In which type of sampling, the parent population is not divided into different groups of strata and all units are treated on the same footing?
(a) Simple Random Sampling
(b) Stratified Random Sampling
(c) Systematic Sampling

500. Circular diagrams are sometimes known as:
(a) Wheel diagrams (b) Pillar diagrams
(c) Block diagrams

CATALOGUING

501. If there are two or more kinds of collaborators, which connecting symbol is used in between two kinds of collaborators in CCC?
   (a) Colon (:) (b) Semi colon (;)
   (c) Dash (-)

502. In case of series what will be the place of 'Number' series in Series Index Entry in CCC?
   (a) In between first and second index
   (b) After series on leading line
   (c) After edition statement

503. If there are two independent series, what will be the sequence of both the series?
   (a) Both series in one circular bracket
   (b) Both series in separate circular brackets
   (c) None of them

504. The word 'and others' is used against the name of the personal author in CCC, if:
   (a) There are two authors
   (b) There are three or more authors
   (c) Neither (a) nor (b)

505. What is the place of collaborators in main entry according to CCC?
   (a) After title (b) After edition (c) After series

506. If there are two collaborators of the same kind, which connecting word/symbol will be used between them?
   (a) Or (b) And (c) Comma (,)

507. What will be the connecting symbol between the author and title in a collaborator index entry in CCC?
   (a) Comma (,) (b) Fullstop (.) (c) Colon (:)

508. The second edition of AACR contains complete scheme for the description of library material based on:
   (a) ISBN (b) ISBD (c) ISSN

509. POPSI has a basic version known as:
(a) POPSI-Basic (b) POPSI-Base
(c) Basic POPSI

510. POPSI process is completed in:
(a) Six steps (b) Seven steps (c) Eight steps

511. Discipline (C), Entity (E), Action (A) and Property (P) are elementary categories of basic principles of:
(a) PRECIS (b) POPSI (c) Search list

512. Which term has been given to the sources for faceted classification in POPSI?
(a) Class roots (b) Class base (c) Class Role operators

513. In POPSI system all the index entries including references are arranged in the sequence of:
(a) Letter-by-letter (b) Word-by-word
(c) Gestalt system

514. Display of POPSI index entries has got similarity with:
(a) KWIC index (b) KWOC index
(c) MEDLAR

515. Who devised the PRECIS?
(a) Derek Austin (b) G. Bhattacharya (c) LC

516. When did BNB decide to use the mark tapes for the first time?
(a) 1967 (b) 1968 (c) 1969

517. BNB introduced PRECIS in:
(a) 1969 (b) 1970 (c) 1971

518. Main line operators, interposed operators and differencing operators are Role Operators, of:
(a) POPSI (b) PRECIS (c) Chain Indexing

519. PRECIS has context dependency and is organised into a context-dependent order:
(a) A > B > C > D (b) A > D > C > B
(c) B > A > C > D

520. Which are three parts of PRECIS entry in standard format of PRECIS?
   (a) Lead, qualifier, display
   (b) Format, qualifier, term
   (c) Lead, display, characteristic

521. The syntax of POPSI system is governed by the principle of context dependency called:
   (a) Priori (b) Posteriori (c) None of them

522. Semantic relations of POPSI are independent of documents called:
   (a) Priori (b) Posteriori (c) Neither of them

523. Which abstract in India prepared its index using PRECIS in 1978?
   (a) Indian Science Abstract
   (b) Indian Library Science Abstract
   (c) Indian Periodical Abstract

524. When did BNB and INB adopt PRECIS?
   (a) 1974 / 1975 (b) 1972 / 1973
   (c) 1975 / 1976

525. In which canon a characteristic used as the basis for the classification of a universe should be relevant to the purpose of classification?
   (a) Canon of differentiation
   (b) Canon of ascertainability
   (c) Canon of relevance

526. In which canon a characteristic used as the basis for the classification of a universe should be definite and ascertainable?
   (a) Canon of permanence
   (b) Canon of relevance
   (c) Canon of ascertainability

527. In which canon a characteristic used as the basis for the classification of a universe should continue to be

unchanged so long as there is no change in the purpose of classification?

(a) Canon of differentiation

(b) Canon of relevance

(c) Canon of permanence

(d) Canon of ascertainability

528. Which notation is a kind of symbolic language depends extensively on memory of meaning or it is a memory aid?

(a) Sector notation (b) Array
(c) Chain (d) Mnemonics

529. Who developed INDONET?

(a) INFLIBNET (b) NIC
(c) CMC (d) CSIR

530. How many indentions are used in a cataloguing entry?

(a) Two (b) Three (c) One (d) Four

531. How many spaces are left for use of 1st, 2nd and 3rd indentions in a typewritten card?

(a) 7-10-12 (b) 8-12-4
(c) 10-12-14 (d) 6-8-10

532. From which line does call number begin in typewritten card in CCC?

(a) 3rd line counting from the top

(b) 2nd line counting from the top

(c) Left edge of leading line

533. Which symbol is used when any information is found from sources other than title page?

(a) Parentheses (b) Circular brackets
(c) Square brackets

534. Where is title of the document located for the purpose of catalogue entry?

(a) Title and half title page

(b) Cover & spine of a book

(c) Bibliography
(d) All locations a, b, c

535. What will you treat if title page is spread in two pages?
(a) Consider first page (b) Consider second page
(c) Treat both page as one

536. If there is no title in a title page where is title located?
(a) Bibliography (b) Back of a book
(c) Any other source like bibliographics

537. Which title is considered if the book is multivolumed having separate titles of the volumes?
(a) Select the last volume title
(b) Select any title of volumes
(c) Select the first title

538. Which book was written by Paul Otlet on documentation?
(a) *Deal de Documentation*
(b) *Book de Documentation*
(c) *Trait de Documentation*

539. Which book was written by S.C. Bradford in 1948?
(a) *Librarianship* (b) *Documentation*
(c) *Document and Library*

540. Which journal is published by ASLIB?
(a) *Documentation*
(b) *Journal of Documentation*
(c) *Journal of Library and Documentation*

541. Who coined the term 'INFORMATICS' in 1966?
(a) U.S.A. (b) Russia (c) France

542. Which subject indexing system uses two principles: 'one to one relationship' and 'context dependency'?
(a) POPSI (b) PRECIS (c) Sears' list

543. Identify full form of KWAC:
(a) Key-word-augumented-in-context
(b) Key-word-automatic-in-context
(c) Key-word-context of augumentation

544. Identify the full form of KWWC:
   (a) Key-word-with-context
   (b) Key-word-without-context
   (c) Key-word-within-context

545. What is the other name of Description Abstracts?
   (a) Indicative (b) Informative (c) Imaginative

546. In which case copyright author is treated as author?
   (a) If there is original author
   (b) If there is additional author
   (c) If there is no author on title page

547. Who will be treated as author if there are more than three authors?
   (a) First author (b) Last author
   (c) No author (d) Title as author

548. Which edition is considered for entry element?
   (a) First edition (b) Last edition
   (c) Last revised edition (d) First revised edition

549. How will we enter 3rd revised edition in entry element?
   (a) 3rd edition (b) Third revised edition
   (c) 3rd revised ed. (d) 3rd rev. ed.

550. Which area consists of publication and printing details like place, date and name of publication in AACR?
   (a) Publisher area
   (b) Imprint
   (c) Distribution area
   (d) Publication/Distribution area

551. When is Series Statement enclosed circular bracket?
   (a) If found on title page
   (b) If not found on title page
   (c) If found on additional or half title page

552. Which statement contains additional information given in the body of the entry?
   (a) Note statement (b) Collation statement
   (c) Series statement

553. In which statement are quotations, phrases composed by cataloguer, entered?
   (a) Bibliographical notes (b) Full content notes
   (c) Partial content notes

554. Where is author statement entered in dictionary catalogue?
   (a) Leading line (b) Below leading line
   (c) Under title statement

555. Which symbol is used after completion of author statement?
   (a) Semicolon (;) (b) Colon (:)
   (c) Fullstop (.) (d) Bracket ([ ])

556. How many spaces are left in between the two abbreviations, if the fore name of the personal author is in abbreviations?
   (a) 5 spaces (b) 6 spaces
   (c) 8 spaces (d) 10 spaces

557. Which statement is followed after author statement?
   (a) Distribution/publication statement
   (b) Series statement
   (c) Collaboration statement
   (d) Title statement

558. From which indention does the title start in the main entry?
   (a) First indention (b) Second indention
   (c) Third indention

559. What is entry location of statement of responsibility?
   (a) After title statement
   (b) After author statement
   (c) After publication responsibility

560. Which symbol is used to attach 'statement of responsibility' with title statement?

(a) Comma (b) Fullstop
(c) Semicolon (d) Slash

561. What is sequence of 'statement of responsibility', i.e. name of the persons?

(a) Surname - Forename (b) Forename - Surname

562. What is sequence of 'statement of responsibility', if names of the persons bear initials or abbreviations?

(a) Comma (b) Fullstop
(c) Slash (d) Semicolon

563. What do you mean by subsequence author/s or collaborators?

(a) The proper author

(b) Authors or persons other than proper author

(c) Authors or persons as subsequent authors, other than the main or the first persons

564. What type of authors are editors, joint authors, translators, compilors, illustrators, etc.?

(a) Proper authors (b) Main authors
(c) Subsequence authors or collaborators

565. If there are two authors, which articles are used to connect them?

(a) 'with' (b) 'and' (c) 'also'

566. If there are three authors, which symbols and articles are used to connect them?

(a) Comma between first two and 'and' between second and third authors

(b) 'and' between first, second and third author

(c) Semicolon between them

567. Which type of numericals are used for numbers of edition statement?

(a) Alphabets (b) Roman (c) Arabic

568. Which type of numericals are used for numbers of edition statement?
    (a) Place of publication
    (b) Name of publisher or printer
    (c) Year of publication
    (d) Place, name & year of publication

569. Which area/statement is entered for the physical features of a document?
    (a) Publication statement
    (b) Collaborator statement
    (c) Note section
    (d) Physical description area

570. What are three types of descriptions entered in Physical Description Area?
    (a) Extent of items/volumes/tapes
    (b) Extent of items/dimension, area/size
    (c) Extent of items/pagination area/dimension (size) area

571. Series is divided in how many parts?
    (a) Two parts (b) Three parts
    (c) Four parts (d) Five parts

572. What is the sequence of four parts of series statement?
    (a) Sub-series/number of series/proper series/edition of series area
    (b) Proper series/sub-series/edition of series area/number of series
    (c) Editor of series/area proper series/sub-series/number of series

573. If all the works by one person appear under one pseudonym and if real name is known, under which name author entry is made?
    (a) Personal author
    (b) Corporate author
    (c) Pseudonymous author

574. When was the Classified Catalogue Code introduced first?
(a) 1936 (b) 1937 (c) 1938 (d) 1939

575. Which is the latest edition of Classified Catalogue Code?
(a) Edition 3 (b) Edition 4
(c) Edition 5 (d) Edition 2

576. In which edition of Classified Catalogue Code, rules of law of symmetry, centralized cataloguing, and conventional documents are included?
(a) Edition 2 (b) Edition 3
(c) Edition 4 (d) Edition 5

577. In which edition of Classified Catalogue Code, rules for union catalogue of periodical publication are included?
(a) Edition 1 (b) Edition 2
(c) Edition 3 (d) Edition 4

578. Which nine capital alphabets constitute an approach of the subject in CCC?
(a) ABCDEFGH & J (b) ACDEFGHI & J
(c) ABCDFGHI & J

579. Which 10 parts (capital alphabets) represent or give the substantive rules for cataloguing?
(a) KLMNPURST & U (b) KLMNOPQRS & U
(c) KLMNPQRST & U

580. What is proper term of the specific normative principles applicable to cataloguing?
(a) Principles (b) Guidelines
(c) Characteristics (d) Canons

581. Which canon directs that information found in the title page of the document catalogued and its overflow pages should determine the choice and rendering of each section of main entry, CRE, book index entry, class index entry, etc.?
(a) Canon of currency
(b) Canon of ascertainability
(c) Canon of sought-heading

582. Which canon applies potency to decide the position of entry, entry elements, leading section?
    (a) Canon of prepotence
    (b) Canon of individualization
    (c) Canon of sought heading

583. Which canon directs the usage of current item to denote a subject in a class index entry of classified catalogue and in a subject entry of a Dictionary Catalogue?
    (a) Canon of prepotence
    (b) Canon of sought heading
    (c) Canon of currency

584. Which type of forms are card form, microforms, etc.?
    (a) Inner forms (b) Physical forms
    (c) Neither (a) nor (b)

585. Which kind of cataloguing consists of Printed card system and Parental cataloguing?
    (a) Cooperative cataloguing
    (b) Centralised cataloguing
    (c) Selected cataloguing

586. The language of cataloguing in which the majority of the documents of a library occur is called:
    (a) Non-favoured language (b) Favoured language

587. What type of card system is known, if main card is copied for added entries adding their specific headings on the top of the card?
    (a) Printed card system (b) Unit card system

588. Which type of written fluid, ink, pencil, chemical or coloured instrument is used to write the call number?
    (a) Ink pen (b) Pencil (c) Fluid

589. Which is the topmost horizontal line of a card?
    (a) Heading line (b) Leading line
    (c) First vertical line

590. Which is the leftmost vertical line of card?
   (a) Second vertical line (b) First vertical line
591. Which is the vertical line which is to the right of first vertical?
   (a) Second vertical line (b) First vertical line
592. What is the location of accession number section at first vertical in CCC?
   (a) Bottommost line
   (b) Last but the bottommost line
   (c) Third onward to bottommost line
593. If there are both personal and corporate authors who will be considered as main author?
   (a) If book deals with functions and purpose of the corporate body which is chiefly responsible for the thoughts and its subject knowledge, then the corporate author.
   (b) Only corporate author
   (c) Only personal author
594. Do 'conferences' come under corporate author?
   (a) Yes (b) No
595. Which form of the name of an institution is used as heading of entry element in CCC?
   (a) Entry element in word or word group denoting the subject
   (b) Entry element in word or word group denoting the first part of corporate body
   (c) Entry element in word or word group
596. If there is personal author and translator both, who will be treated as chief author?
   (a) Personal author (b) Translator (c) Both
597. Is call number written in pencil in each entry?
   (a) Yes (b) No

598. In how many parts the tracing part is divided in CCC?
   (a) One part (b) Two parts (c) Four parts

599. From where do sections start first vertical in CCC?
   (a) Call number and series
   (b) Call number and author
   (c) Call number and accession number

600. When is collaborator treated as heading in the author statement?
   (a) When author is not well known
   (b) When there is no author
   (c) When only the collaborator is given

601. Who would be considered author of the following dependent authors in CCC — (a) Paraphrase (b) Abridgement (c) Adaptation?
   (a) Dependent author
   (b) Original author of the work
   (c) Title

602. Which punctuation mark is used to separate blocks (or word groups) in a heading in CCC?
   (a) Semicolon (b) Fullstop (c) Comma

603. Why is individualizing element used?
   (a) To separate the irrelevant part of heading
   (b) To give more importance to special part of heading
   (c) To resolve homonym to individualize the entity

604. What is the main entry?
   (a) Which gives important information
   (b) Which gives maximum information about the document
   (c) Which has all bibliographical information

605. What is a multifocal book?
   (a) Which deals with one subject
   (b) Which deals with two subjects
   (c) Which deals with more than one subject

606. Which type of handwriting has been suggested by S.R. Ranganathan for entry?
   (a) Ordinary hand (b) Italic handwriting
   (c) Library hand

607. What is the purpose of guide card in catalogue?
   (a) To indicate the good display
   (b) To support the catalogue cards
   (c) To indicate the arrangement of filing the cards

608. What is handing indention?
   (a) Which is third imaginary indention
   (b) Which starts the title entry
   (c) There is no handing indention

609. What was the earlier name of Canon sought heading?
   (a) Canon of prepotency (b) Canon of command
   (c) Canon of relevance

610. What is 'Alternate title'?
   (a) Second dependent title (b) Subtitle
   (c) Equivalent title

611. What is continued card?
   (a) The second card
   (b) The card used for additional information
   (c) The card which continues an entry from a preceding card

612. What are the directing words?
   (a) Which are used in each entry
   (b) Which are used as individualizing element
   (c) Which direct the reader to see from one heading to another

613. What is secondary element?
   (a) The element supplementing the author
   (b) The element used for heading
   (c) The element other than entry element and the individualizing element

614. What is a sub-series?
   (a) Which is additional series
   (b) Which is subordinate series
   (c) Which is alternative series

615. What is Annotation?
   (a) A summary of a book
   (b) A bibliographical description of a book
   (c) Special features of a book

616. What is fanciful title?
   (a) Which supports the main title
   (b) Which indicates the special features of the title
   (c) Which does not disclose the subject of the book

617. What is meant by subject catalogue?
   (a) A catalogue of subjects
   (b) A division of subjects for catalogue
   (c) A catalogue consisting of subject entries

618. What is meant by new edition?
   (a) The edition of new book
   (b) The first edition of a book
   (c) The edition which differs from the previous one

619. What is a compound name?
   (a) The name with two surnames
   (b) More than one name
   (c) The name consists of two or more proper names connected by a hyphen, preposition, or conjunction

620. Who used decimal fraction notation for arrangement of books?
   (a) C.A. Cutter (b) Melvil Dewey
   (c) S.R. Ranganathan

621. What is alternative term of Analytico synthetic classification?
   (a) Freely faceted classification
   (b) Faceted classification
   (c) Rigid classification

622. From which Latin word has the term Classification been derived?
   (a) Calassis (b) Calssis (c) Classis

623. Who worked as a Student Library Assistant in Amherst College?
   (a) H.E. Bliss (b) S.R. Ranganathan
   (c) Melvil Dewey

624. Who formulated principles of scientific and educational consensus?
   (a) H.E. Bliss (b) Melvil Dewey
   (c) S.R. Ranganathan

625. What is sequence of planes of S.R. Ranganathan?
   (a) Notational plane, idea plane, verbal plane
   (b) Verbal plane, notational plane, idea plane
   (c) Idea plane, verbal plane, notational plane

626. Which theory has been formulated by J.D. Brown, an English classificationist which is practiced in three classification schemes?
   (a) 'One subject' theory
   (b) 'Two place theory' of one subject
   (c) 'One place theory' for all subjects

627. Who published *Bibliotheca Bibliographic Classification* in 30 volumes?
   (a) VINITY, Moscow
   (b) Central Library, Moscow
   (c) Lavin Library of Congress, Moscow

628. Who devised 'International Classification Scheme' in 1961?
   (a) E.C. Richardson (b) J.D. Brown
   (c) Fremont Rider

629. How many pages were there in DDC during 1876?
   (a) 38 pages (b) 48 pages (c) 52 pages

630. Who devised 'A Bibliographic Classification extended by systematic auxiliary schedules' during 1940-1953?
   (a) H.E. Bliss (b) S.R. Ranganathan
   (c) J.D. Brown

631. Is Rider's International Classification an enumerative scheme of classification?
   (a) Yes (b) No

632. Which term has E.C. Richardson given to notations?
   (a) Type-written sign (b) Mixed sign
   (c) Shorthand sign

633. How many zones were recognized by Dr. S.R. Ranganathan?
   (a) Two (b) Three (c) Four (d) Five

634. Which classification did not follow Mnemonics?
   (a) Knowledge classification
   (b) Bibliographical classification
   (c) LC classification

635. Which levels were deleted in 7th edition of colon classification?
   (a) Personality levels (b) Matter levels
   (c) Matter and space levels (d) Space and time levels

636. How many modes have been formed by Ranganathan for formation of subject in the universe of knowledge?
   (a) Three (b) Four (c) Five

637. What is an ultimate class?
   (a) Class with longer extension
   (b) Class with smaller extension
   (c) Class with smallest extension

638. What is the indicator digit for common isolates in Expensive Classification of C.A. Cutter?

(a) Colon (b) Semicolon
(c) Dash (d) Dot

639. Who sponsored the formation of 'Library Research Circle in India' in Delhi in Sept. 1961?

(a) G. Bhattacharya (b) P.N. Kewla
(c) S.R. Ranganathan

640. Who invented 'retroactive ordinal notation'?

(a) H.E. Bliss (b) E.J. Coates
(c) S.R. Ranganathan

641. Which edition of DDC was edited by Benjamin A. Custer?

(a) Ed. 16-19 (b) Ed. 17-18 (c) Ed. 16-20

642. Which journal is published by DRTC, Bangalore?

(a) *Library Herald*
(b) *Herald of Library Science*
(c) *Library Science with a Slant to Documentation* (SRELS Journal of Information Management)

643. When was the journal *Library Science with Slant to Documentation* started?

(a) 1962 (b) 1963 (c) 1964

644. Indicate the 'facet formula':

(a) MESTP (b) PEMST (c) PMEST

645. What is the size of standard catalogue card?

(a) 5″ × 3″ (b) 5¼′ × 2¾′
(c) 12.5 × 7.5cm

646. What is standard thickness size of catalogue card?

(a) 0.025 (b) 0.030 (c) 0.022 (d) 0.02

647. In which catalogue the corporate names are treated as subjects of a book?

(a) Author catalogue (b) Name catalogue
(c) Subject catalogue

648. Indicate such card system which is prepared in the form of main entry and duplicated for using the headings of other added entries:
   (a) Abridged card system (b) Main card system
   (c) Unit card system

649. In which catalogue code, both types of catalogues—classified part and dictionary part are covered?
   (a) AACR-II (b) L.C. Catalogue Code
   (c) Classified Catalogue Code

650. Who has started the dictionary catalogue as "the least simple and most confusing"?
   (a) C.A. Cutter (b) S.R. Ranganathan
   (c) H.E. Bliss

651. Which side of catalogue card is used for tracing purpose in classified catalogue?
   (a) Front side (b) Upper side (c) Back side

652. In which section the tracing is entered in main entry in dictionary catalogue AACR-II?
   (a) Last section (b) Note section
   (c) Content note (d) Tracing section

653. What is proper sequence of entries in tracing in AACR-II?
   (a) Subject→joint authors→collaborators→title→series
   (b) Subject→collaborators→series entries
   (c) Joint authors→collaborators→title→series→subject entries

654. Which type of notations are used for putting serial number for subject entries?
   (a) Roman capital (b) Roman small
   (c) Indo-Arabic numerals

655. In which side of tracing section, the added entries are referred by their headings?
   (a) Left side (b) Right side (c) Central place

656. In which side the tracing entries of serials are referred in tracing section?

(a) Left side (b) Right side (c) Central place

657. What is the sequence of statement of serials entered in tracing section?

(a) Year→Accession No.→Book No.→Volume No.

(b) Volume No.→Book No.→Year→Accession No.

(c) Volume No.→Year→Book No.→Accession No.

658. What is the place of cross reference index entries in tracing section of CCC?

(a) Top (b) Middle (c) Bottom

659. What is the place of subject entries in tracing section of CCC?

(a) Top (b) Middle (c) Bottom

660. In case of tracing in CCC, what is the position of 'hole' of the catalogue card?

(a) Upper side (b) Lower side
(c) Towards the middle

661. What do we call secondary entries in AACR-II?

(a) Main entry (b) Book index entries
(c) Added entries

662. Which is the latest physical form of library catalogue?

(a) Card form (b) Magnetic tapes
(c) Computers

663. What is proper name of loose-leaf form among physical forms of catalogue?

(a) Book form (b) Punched card form
(c) Card form (d) Sheaf form

664. Which cataloguing includes selective cataloguing and simplified cataloguing?

(a) Dictionary cataloguing (b) Union cataloguing
(c) Limited cataloguing

665. In which cataloguing a number of independent libraries join together and share all the responsibilities including finance for mutual benefits?

(a) Centralised cataloguing

(b) Cooperative cataloguing

(c) Selective cataloguing

666. What is the contribution of Anthony Panizzi in the field of Authorship?

(a) Personal authorship

(b) Corporate authorship

(c) Serials

667. Who used the term 'Pre-Natal Catalgouing' for the first time?

(a) E.C. Richardson (b) A Neelameghan
(c) S.R. Ranganathan

668. What signs or symbols are used for entries of individualizing element in CCC?

(a) Inverted commas (b) Square bracket
(c) Circular bracket

669. What signs or symbols are used for entries if information is found from outside sources?

(a) Circular bracket (b) Square bracket
(c) Inverted commas

670. Is publication statement given in CCC?

(a) Yes (b) No

671. Who devised ISBD?

(a) IFLA (b) FIP (c) UNESCO

672. When was the 'Canon of Recall Value' propounded by S.R. Ranganathan?

(a) 1968 (b) 1969 (c) 1970

673. How many laws of Library Science were enunciated by S.R. Ranganathan?

(a) Three (b) Four (c) Five (d) Six

674. With which name the Normative Principles are also known in CCC?

(a) Laws (b) Postulates (c) Canons

675. Which statement consists of the statement of joint authors and collaborators' statement in AACR-II?

(a) Title statement (b) Author statement
(c) Edition statement

676. If there are three authors of a book, how many authors are to be considered for entry element in heading section of CCC?

(a) One (b) Two (c) Three

677. If the book is a 'fifth edition', how will it be entered in edition statement in main entry of CCC?

(a) Edition 5th (b) 5th edition
(c) 5th ed. (d) Ed. 5

678. How is edition given in edition statement if the book is seventh edition, in main entry in AACR-II?

(a) Edition seventh (b) Ed. 7th
(c) 7th Ed.

679. What will be the connecting symbol if there are two types of collaborators, in AACR-II?

(a) : (Colon) (b) . (Fullstop)
(c) ; (Semicolon) (d) — (Dash)

680. What symbol is used in author statement if author is written after title, in AACR-II?

(a) — (Dash) (b) : (Colon)
(c) / (Slash)

681. Is series written in continuation of physical description, in AACR-II?

(a) No (b) Yes

682. Is series written in continuation of edition section, in CCC?

(a) Yes (b) No

683. If the page gives only a pseudonym in place of the author's name, what descriptive element is written with the heading in CCC?

(a) Psend (b) Pseudonym (c) Pseud

684. In which handwriting the statements of heading of tracing are written in CCC?

(a) Capital letters Roman (b) Small Roman letters
(c) In abbreviations (d) Ordinary hand

685. What will be entry element on leading line in cross reference entry in CCC?

(a) Heading of heading section
(b) Call number of the book
(c) Class number of the book

686. Who devised chain procedure?

(a) C.A. Cutter (b) H.E. Bliss
(c) S.R. Ranganathan

687. What we call the link, which is not a class number in chain procedure?

(a) Last link (b) Missing link (c) False link

688. What is that link which occurs last in the chain produced by a class number in chain procedure?

(a) Missing link (b) False link (c) Last link

689. Which is that link, which ends with a part of the isolate focus in a facet of a class number in chain procedure?

(a) Sought link (b) Missing link
(c) False link (d) Unsought link

690. Indicate the link which is neither false, nor fused nor unsought and links ending with an aftertime Auteriorising Common Isolate Digit:

(a) Upper link (b) Unsought link
(c) Sought link (d) False link

691. Indicate the link, which is a link in a chain-with-gap corresponding to the missing isolate in the chain in chain procedure:

(a) False link (b) Last link (c) Missing link

692. Which link is used as entry element for class index entry in CCC?

(a) Unsought links (b) False links
(c) Sought links

693. How many words contain their first letter in capital while writing the directing words in class index entries in CCC?

(a) 5 (b) 6 (c) 7 (d) 8

694. What do we name the call number when it is written in the end of the added entries and class index entries in CXCC?

(a) Call number (b) Index number

695. Which corporate body is entered with its Territory in CCC and AACR-II?

(a) Conference (b) Institutions
(c) Government

696. Whether initial articles are to be written in rendering the name of an institution in CCC?

(a) Yes (b) No

697. Which words are to be omitted, if found either to the beginning or at the end, while rendering the name of an institution in CCC?

(a) Italic words (b) Honorific words

698. In which form the number is to be written, if the name of an institution begins with a numeral figure?

(a) Speltout in language (b) In numerals
(c) Omitted

699. Which entry will be made in case of change of name of an institution in CCC?

(a) Cross reference entry
(b) Cross reference index entry
(c) Added entry

700. What will be position of the name of the place of a diplomatic conference, to the name of the conference not held periodically?
(a) Suffixed (b) Prefixed
(c) Below the name of the conference

701. What type of heading will there be, if a conference is the organ of another corporate body in CCC?
(a) Main heading (b) Multiple corporate heading
(c) Parent body heading

702. What is full form of ICCP, held in Paris?
(a) International conference on cataloguing practice
(b) International conference on classification principles
(c) Indian conference of cataloguing principles
(d) International conference on cataloguing principles

703. What is full form of IFLA?
(a) Indian Federation of Library Association
(b) International Federation of Library Association
(c) International Formation of Library Associates
(d) Indian Foundation of Library Associations

704. ICCP conference was held in Paris in the year:
(a) 1960 (b) 1963 (c) 1961 (c) 1965

705. What is full form of MARC?
(a) Machine added readable course
(b) Machine readable catalogue
(c) Machine advance research code
(d) Machine readable code

706. Anglo-American cataloguing rules were first published in:
(a) 1968 (b) 1967 (c) 1966 (d) 1970

707. What is full form of S.R. Ranganathan?
(a) Shivram Ramanuj Ranganathan
(b) Shiyali Ramamrit Ranganathan

(c) Shrima, Ramamrit Ranganathan
(d) Shri Ram Ranganathan

708. In Dewey Decimal Classification, 9 is used as:
(a) Sectorising digit (b) Sectional digit
(c) Subject digit (d) Sub-division digit

709. 'Cata Logos' is a/an:
(a) Arabic phrase (b) Urdu phrase
(c) Greek phrase (d) French phrase

710. Cataloger is a person who:
(a) Prepares catalogue (b) Maintains catalogue
(c) Prints catalogue (d) Publishes catalogue

711. C.A. Cutter's full name is:
(a) Chancer Agnes Cutter
(b) Charles Albert Cutter
(c) Charles Ami Cutter
(d) Charlic Anglo Cutter

712. C.A. Cutter enunciated:
(a) Regulations for dictionary catalogue
(b) Rules for a dictionary catalogue
(c) Rules for a dictionary code
(d) Rules for a direct catalogue

713. British Library Association is abbreviated as:
(a) BLA (b) LA (c) BRLA (d) BLAS

714. What is full form of ALA?
(a) Anglo-Library Association
(b) Abgila Library Association
(c) American Library Association
(d) Allied Library Association

715. What is full form of CCC?
(a) Class-wise Catalogue Code
(b) Classified Catalogue Code

(c) Chronological Classified Code

(d) Classified Classification Code

716. Classified catalogue code is introduced by:

(a) C.A. Cutter (b) American Library Association
(c) S.R. Ranganathan (d) Melvil Dewey

717. Standard catalogue card has a size of:

(a) 3″ × 5″ (b) 7.5cm × 12.5cm
(c) 3.5″ × 5.5″ (d) 7cm × 12cm

718. Thickness of standard catalogue card is:

(a) 0.030cm (b) 0.035cm
(c) 0.025 (d) 0.027cm

719. Which is the last section of main entry?

(a) Note section (b) Content section
(c) Tracing section (d) Series section

720. Which reference entry directs the user from one heading to a related heading?

(a) See-reference entry

(b) See also reference entry

(c) Subject reference entry

(d) Also see reference entry

721. Which reference entry directs the user from the name of a person or a corporate body or the title of work or subject or name of series which the user looks to the form chosen by cataloguer?

(a) See-also-reference entry

(b) See-reference entry

(c) Serial reference entry

(d) Subject reference entry

722. When was 'Sears' list of subject heading' first published?

(a) 1927 (b) 1925 (c) 1923 (d) 1924

723. ALA committee on index to subject heading was formed in:

(a) 1901 (b) 1890 (c) 1892 (d) 1895

724. ALA list of subject heading for use in dictionary catalogue was brought out in:

(a) 1894 (b) 1895 (c) 1896 (d) 1898

725. Which is National Library of America (U.S.A.)?

(a) Central Library of Washington
(b) National Library of America
(c) Library of Congress
(d) National Library of Congress

726. What is the full form of POPSI?

(a) Postulate permuted subject heading
(b) Postulate based permuted subject heading
(c) Postulate permuted serial heading
(d) Postulate based pre-subject heading

727. What is full form of PRECIS?

(a) Preserved context indexing system
(b) Postulate context indexing system
(c) Preserved common indexing system
(d) Preserved context index system

728. Which is the name of national bibliography of United Kingdom?

(a) U.K. National Bibliography
(b) National Bibliography of U.K.
(c) British National Bibliography
(d) Britain National Bibliography

729. In which year BNB started following PRECIS?

(a) 1969 (b) 1970 (c) 1971 (d) 1972

730. What is full form of DRTC?

(a) Documentation Record Training Centre
(b) Department of Research Training Centre
(c) Documentation Research Training Centre
(d) Document Research Training Centre

731. How many cataloguing rules were laid down by Anthony Panizzi?
(a) 79 (b) 90 (c) 91 (d) 92

732. Which library was headed by Anthony Panizzi as Librarian?
(a) Library of Congress
(b) Indian National Library
(c) National Library of Australia
(d) British Museum

733. How many rules of Panizzi were reduced in its revised edition?
(a) 85 (b) 71 (c) 41 (d) 5

734. In which year was Charles C. Jewett's code for the catalogue of the Smithsonian Institution accepted?
(a) 1872 (b) 1876 (c) 1874 (d) 1875

735. Which catalogue code was compiled by Vatican Library in 1927?
(a) Rules for the catalogue of printed books
(b) Rules for the catalogue of Vatican books
(c) Code of printed books catalogue
(d) Catalogue code of printed books

736. Which catalogue code was introduced in 1934?
(a) Classified catalogue code
(b) Classed catalogue code
(c) Class-based catalogue code
(d) Cooperative catalogue code

737. Who enunciated canons for cataloguing in 1938?
(a) C.A. Cutter (b) K.A. Linderfelt
(c) Charles C. Jewett (d) S.R. Ranganathan

738. In which book Ranganathan introduced canons of cataloguing for the first time?
(a) *Classified Catalogue Code* (1945)
(b) *Theory of Library Catalogue* (1938)

(c) *Dictionary Catalogue Code* (1945)
(d) *Five Laws of Library Science*

739. In which year S.R. Ranganathan introduced Five Laws of Library Science?
(a) 1921 (b) 1930 (c) 1929 (d) 1928

740. Which code was introduced in the year 1908?
(a) ALA code (b) AA code
(c) AACR (d) CCC

741. Who brought out 'Rules for Descriptive Cataloguing' in 1949?
(a) Library Association (U.K.)
(b) American Library Association
(c) Library of Congress
(d) National Library of Australia

742. Which code was published in 1949 in the United States?
(a) AA Code (b) AACR Code
(c) ALA Code (d) Classified Catalogue Code

743. Who is the publisher of the journal "Library Science with a Slant to Documentation."
(a) IASLIC, Kolkata (b) ILA, New Delhi
(c) ALA, New York (d) DRTC, Banglore

744. Which canon of S.R. Ranganathan represents the potency (power and strength) to decide the position of an entry among various entries in a catalogue?
(a) Canon of currency (b) Canon of context
(c) Canon of permanence (d) Canon of prepotency

745. Which canon was propounded by S.R. Ranganathan in 1969?
(a) Canon of ascertainability (b) Canon of currency
(c) Canon of recall value (d) Canon of prepotency

746. Who introduced the 'rules for filing cards' in 1968?
(a) ALA (b) LA (c) ILA (d) CLA

747. Who prepared 'Electric card catalogue rules' in 1890 in Germany?

(a) Karl Dziatzko (b) K.A. Linderfelt
(c) D.M. Norris (d) Charles C. Jewett

748. In which year Library of Congress started printing and selling printed cards?

(a) 1896 (b) 1900 (c) 1899 (d) 1901

749. How many rules were propounded by Charles C. Jewett in its 'Jewett Catalogue Code' in 1852?

(a) 49 rules (b) 39 rules
(c) 51 rules (d) 35 rules

750. In what capacity was Mr. Seymour Lubetzky appointed in American Library Association to revise ALA catalogue code?

(a) Compiler (b) Librarian
(c) Editor (d) Catalogue

751. In which year was AACR-II published?

(a) 1976 (b) 1978 (c) 1980 (d) 1977

752. Of which literature Mr. William D. Cooley, Commissioner of British Museum, prepared the index in 1882?

(a) Periodicals (b) Books
(c) Monographs (d) Manuscripts

753. Which institution issued Cooperative Cataloguing Manual in 1944 in the U.S.A.?

(a) Central Reference Library
(b) Library of Congress
(c) American Library Association
(d) National Medical Library

754. When was the first 'Public Library Act' passed in the United Kingdom?

(a) 1850 (b) 1852 (c) 1856 (d) 1902

755. When did the Prussian libraries prepare Union Catalogue (Author)?

(a) 1930 (b) 1931 (c) 1935 (d) 1938

756. How many categories are there in a subject catalogue?

(a) 2 (b) 3 (c) 3 (d) 5

757. How many 'planes' were introduced (formulated) by S.R. Ranganathan?

(a) 2 (b) 5 (c) 3 (d) 4

758. On which concept is the idea plane based?

(a) Discussion (b) Conversion
(c) Thought (d) Written work

759. On which concept is the verbal plane based?

(a) Written work (b) Numerical
(c) Discussion conversation (d) Thought

760. On which concept is the notational plane based?

(a) Notation (b) Alphabets
(c) Symbols (d) Thoughts

761. Who introduced Gestalt System of alphabetisation

(a) S.R. Ranganathan (b) Melvil Dewey
(c) ALA (d) ILA

762. Which book of S.R. Ranganathan was published in 1938?

(a) *Five Laws of Library Science*
(b) *Classified Catalogue Code*
(c) *Canons and Headings*
(d) *Theory of Library Catalogue*

763. Who wrote the book *Memories of Libraries* in 1859?

(a) Edward Edwards (b) James Cranshaw
(c) C.A. Cutter (d) S.R. Ranganathan

764. Which book of William Warner Bishop was published by Williams and Wilkins in 1924?

(a) *Handbook of Modern Library Cataloguing*
(b) *Handbook of Cataloguing*

(c) *Modern Library Cataloguing*
(d) *A Specific Handbook of Modern Library Cataloguing*

765. Who compiled analytical and classed catalogue of the Brooklyn library in 1881?

(a) S.B. Noyes (b) Henry Bond
(c) A.L.A. (d) Richmond

766. What term is given to the description of printer and publication in ALA catalogue?

(a) Collation (b) Imprint
(c) Tracing (d) Note section

767. What term is given to the statement of the number of volumes/ pages/illustrations, maps and facsimiles in ALA Cataloguing?

(a) Imprint (b) Collation
(c) Series note (d) Note section

768. In which year was sheaf catalogue first practiced?

(a) 1871 (b) 1872 (c) 1875 (d) 1878

769. What size of sheaf catalogue was devised for the first time?

(a) 20.75" × 8" (b) 20.50" × 7.5"
(c) 19.00 " × 7.5 " (d) 20.75 " × 7.5 "

770. What is the capacity of medium weight catalogue cards of size 5" × 3" of a drawer of catalogue cabinet of a size of 17¼?

(a) 1000 (b) 1100 (c) 1200 (d) 950

771. Who prepared 'List of Subject Headings for Small Libraries' in 1933 published by H.W. Wilson Co., New York?

(a) Minnie E. Sears (b) American Library Association
(c) A.C. Cutter (d) Arundell Esdaile

772. What is the term used for the real name of the author?

(a) Antonym (b) Pseudonym
(c) Basic name (d) Main name

773. What is catalogue term used for a name preceding a surname, usually a Christian name?
(a) Nickname (b) Fore name
(c) Real name (d) Artificial name

774. What term is used for the size and shape of a book?
(a) Physical form (b) Book-form
(c) Format (d) Body of a book

775. What term is used for the books printed before 1500?
(a) Incunabula (b) Classics
(c) Manuscripts (d) Rare books

776. What term is used for a book limited to a single subject?
(a) Monograph (b) Classic
(c) Rare book (d) Manuscript

777. In which institute was Charles Jewett librarian in 1950?
(a) Smithsonain Institute
(b) Manchester Public Library
(c) American Library Association
(d) Library Science Bureau of Education, U.S.A.

778. In which year was American Library Association established?
(a) 1876 (b) 1875 (c) 1878 (d) 1902

779. In which year was Library Association of U.K. established?
(a) 1875 (b) 1876 (c) 1877 (d) 1878

780. Which country Melvil Dewey belongs to?
(a) U.K. (b) France (c) U.S.A. (d) Italy

781. Who was the Honorary Secretary of the Library Association's Cataloguing Rules Sub-Committee in 1951?
(a) Seymour Libetzky (b) Summer Splending
(c) Henry A. Sharp (d) Paul S. Dunkin

782. In which year Miss Piggott was Chairman of Descriptive Cataloguing Rules Sub Committee?
(a) 1961 (b) 1962 (c) 1964 (d) 1965

783. In which year was Cutter's Rule for a Dictionary catalogue formulated?

(a) 1901 (b) 1902 (c) 1903 (d) 1904

784. In which year were ALA cataloguing rules, author and title entries formulated?

(a) 1907 (b) 1908 (c) 1909 (d) 1910

785. Which catalogue consists of author, title and subject entries arranged in one alphabetical order?

(a) Name catalogue
(b) Alphabetical subject catalogue
(c) Dictionary catalogue
(d) Classified catalogue

786. Which catalogue arranges the entries in a systematic order of subjects, the order of a classification scheme?

(a) Alphabetical subject catalogue
(b) Classified catalogue
(c) Dictionary catalogue
(d) Author catalogue

787. Which association published rules for filing catalogue cards in 1942?

(a) British Library Association
(b) Canadian Library Association
(c) American Library Association
(d) Indian Library Association

788. Who is the author of the *Popular Libraries of the World*?

(a) S.R. Ranganathan (b) Lawrence S. Thompson
(c) Bostwick (d) Burton

789. Who made planning of Alexandria Library in 283 B.C.?

(a) Toleni Sotter (b) Alexender the Great
(c) Kind of Diodician (d) Plato

790. How many papyrus rolles were housed in Alexendria Library in 4th Century B.C.?
(a) 700,000 (b) 650,000
(c) 720,000 (d) 735,000

791. Where was the first monastic library established in A.D. 529?
(a) Rome (b) Italy (c) England (d) Ireland

792. In which country was the first seminar/departmental library established known as 'Seminarium' libraries in 19th century?
(a) France (b) Italy
(c) England (d) Germany

793. Name the place where "Bibliotheque Nationale" was established in 1480:
(a) Alexandria (b) London
(c) Paris (d) Berlin

794. In which year was 'British Museum' established?
(a) 1753 (b) 1750 (c) 1754 (d) 1751

795. Name the library which was established in Moscow in 1865:
(a) Moscow Library
(b) National Library of U.S.S.R.
(c) VINITY
(d) The Lenin State Library

796. Who inaugurated the UNESCO seminar on the development of public libraries in Asia on Oct. 6, 1995 in India?
(a) Jawaharlal Nehru (b) Dr. Rajendra Prasad
(c) Dr. S. Radhakrishnan
(d) Maulana Abul Kalam Azad

797. In which year first modern library movement in India began in Baroda?
(a) 1910 (b) 1911 (c) 1912 (d) 1914

798. Which was the first early library in Madras founded in 1812?
   (a) Madras Public Library
   (b) Conmera Library
   (c) Madras Library Society
   (d) Madras University Library

799. In which year was the Public Library of Calcutta founded?
   (a) 1835 (b) 1836 (c) 1837 (d) 1839

800. Which library was first started in Bombay in 1846?
   (a) Peoples Library (b) Citizens Library
   (c) Bombay Public Library (d) Our Library

801. Which three University libraries were started in 1857?
   (a) Bombay, Madras, Delhi
   (b) Madras, Bombay, Allahabad
   (c) Bombay, Delhi, Nagpur
   (d) Bombay, Madras, Calcutta

802. Who was the American Librarian invited to India by Maharaja Shivajirao Gaekwad in 1910?
   (a) James Duff (b) Melvil Dewey
   (c) W.A. Borden (d) C.A. Bordon

803. Which committee was appointed by the Govt. of Bombay in 1939 to create a network of public libraries in Maharashtra?
   (a) State Development Committee
   (b) Bombay Library Committee
   (c) Library Development Committee
   (d) Maharashtra Library Committee

804. What was the name of National Library, Calcutta before the present name?
   (a) Imperial Library
   (b) Calcutta Public Library
   (c) Calcutta Public Library
   (d) Peoples Public Library

805. In which building was the Imperial Library, Calcutta functioning?

(a) University Campus (b) Municipal Premises
(c) Town Hall (d) Esplanade Premises

806. What is name of the famous building where National Library, Calcutta is functioning since 1948?

(a) Town Hall (b) Committee Hall
(c) Learning Tower (d) Belvedere

807. In which year was the first delivery of books/public library passed in India?

(a) March, 1952 (b) May, 1954
(c) April, 1953 (d) March, 1953

808. When did the National Library, Calcutta release the first issue of Indian National Bibliography?

(a) Aug. 15, 1958 (b) Oct. 2, 1958
(c) Jan. 26, 1958 (d) Jan. 15, 1958

809. Which public library was first established in Delhi with the assistance of UNESCO in 1951?

(a) Delhi Town Hall Library
(b) John's Public Library
(c) Nizamuddin Public Library
(d) Delhi Public Library

810. Who was the first Indian who went to England to study library science in November, 1924?

(a) B.S. Kesavan (b) Dr. D.V. Roa
(c) Dr. S.R. Ranganathan (d) Dr. J.S. Sharma

811. Which library legislation came into force in Indian states first in 1948?

(a) Bombay Library Act
(b) Mysore Library Legislation
(c) Madras Library Act
(d) Calcutta Library Act

812. Who inaugurated the Gujarat Vidyapith Library on Jan. 5, 1955?
(a) Dr. Rajendra Prasad
(b) Dr. S. Radhakrishnan
(c) Jawaharlal Nehru
(b) Abul Kalam Azad

813. Who was the Chairman of UGC Review Committee, set up in July, 1961?
(a) B.S. Kesavan (b) Dr. K.L. Srimali
(c) Dr. D.S. Kothari (d) Dr. S.R. Ranganathan

814. In which year was Delhi Public Library established?
(a) 1950 (b) 1955 (c) 1951 (d) 1956

815. In which year was 'Indian Library Association' founded?
(a) Sept. 12, 1933 (b) Jan. 11, 1934
(c) Sept. 15, 1933 (d) Dec. 15, 1934

816. In which year was IASLIC (Indian Association of Special Libraries and Information Centre) founded?
(a) Sept. 3, 1955 (b) Jan. 15, 1956
(c) Dec. 11, 1955 (d) Dec. 17, 1956

817. In which year was the first school of Library Science set up in the world at Columbia College, New York?
(a) 1885 (b) 1886 (c) 1887 (d) 1888

818. Who was initiator to start Library Science training in Punjab University in 1915?
(a) Melvil Dewey (b) S.R. Ranganathan
(c) W.A. Borden (d) A.D. Dickinson

819. In which year Delhi University started Library Science Course in its Institute of Library Science?
(a) 1956 (b) 1957 (c) 1958 (d) 1959

820. In which year was INSDOC (Indian National Documentation Centre) set up in New Delhi?
(a) 1951 (b) 1952 (c) 1953 (d) 1954

821. When was DRTC (Document Research and Training Centre) established in India at Bangalore?
(a) Aug. 10, 1962 (b) Aug. 18, 1962
(c) Dec. 11, 1963 (d) Jan. 5, 1964

822. Who was the Chairman of UGC Library Committee set up in 1958?
(a) S.R. Ranganathan (b) Dr. D.S. Kothari
(c) B.S. Kesavan (d) P.N. Karla

823. Which catalogue is arranged alphabetically by name of persons, places?
(a) Author catalogue
(b) Name catalogue
(c) Classified catalogue
(d) Alphabetico classed catalogue

824. Which is a full catalogue entry, usually the author entry and called master card?
(a) Added entry (b) Shelflist entry
(c) Main entry (d) Subject entry

825. Who first suggested to adopt Inter-library loan in 1876?
(a) S.S. Green (b) Melvil Dewey
(c) S.R. Ranganathan (d) C.A. Cutter

826. In which year ALA set up a code for Inter-Library loan?
(a) 1916 (b) 1917 (c) 1918 (d) 1919

827. Which library started Inter-library loan service in India in 1903?
(a) Conmera Library
(b) Madras University Library
(c) National Library Calcutta
(d) Delhi University Library

828. Who contributed Bibliographic Classification in U.S.A. in 1935?
(a) H.E. Bliss (b) Ian Robert
(c) W.W. Bishop (d) S.T. Coleridge

829. Which term we use to refer to old issues of journals?
(a) Classics (b) Rare issues
(c) Back volumes (d) Issues not published

830. What do you call the card representing a book, which is kept in front or back cover?
(a) Borrower card (b) Shelflist card
(c) Catalogue card (d) Book card

831. What do you call the number which distinguishes a book from others lying on the shelf?
(a) Call number (b) Class number
(c) Book number (d) Accession number

832. What do you call the card representing a borrower, containing all information about borrower?
(a) Book card (b) Catalogue card
(c) Borrower card (d) Index card

833. What do you call a joint number for classification and book number?
(a) Book number (b) Class number
(c) Accession number (d) Call number

834. Analytical entry is prepared for:
(a) Alternative title (b) Full document
(c) Part of the document (d) None of the above

835. Which system is devised by U.S. National Library of Medicine, which records on magnetic tape indexes of Biomedical articles?
(a) MEDLARS (b) MARC-II
(c) KWOC (d) KWIC

836. Which type of Mnemonics are known as seminal Mnemonics?
(a) Scheduled Mnemonics
(b) Unscheduled Mnemonics
(c) None of them

837. What is the full name of Berwick Sayers?
   (a) William Berwick Sayers
   (b) William Charles Sayers
   (c) William Charles Berwick Sayers

838. What do you call the secluded place in library for study and doing research?
   (a) Reference Cell (b) Study Cell
   (c) Research Cell (d) Carrells

839. Which IIT library was first established in India?
   (a) Delhi (b) Gauhati
   (c) Bombay (d) Kharagpur

REFERENCE SERVICE

840. Xerographic process is categorized under:
   (a) Photographic process
   (b) Reflex method
   (c) Silver halide process
   (d) Electrostatic process

841. Which is a literary composition in journals?
   (a) Bibliography (b) Chapters
   (c) Articles (d) Volumes

842. What do you call 'A volume of maps'?
   (a) Map (b) Atlas
   (c) Geographic Plates (d) Diagrams

843. The *Study Abroad* is a/an:
   (a) Encyclopedia (b) Yearbook
   (c) Directory (d) Handbook

844. The 'user profile' is a:
   (a) List of descriptors
   (b) List of useful citations
   (c) List of users
   (d) Statement on user information

845. Phoenix schedules are part of:
(a) DDC (b) BC (c) UDC (d) LCC

846. Which term is used for a size of book whose printing paper is folded into sheets of 16 pages?
(a) Recto (b) Octavo
(c) Quarter page (d) Full page

847. Which term is used for the size of book when its printing paper is folded into 4 sheets or 8 pages?
(a) Recto (b) Octavo
(c) Quarto (d) Quarter page

848. Which term is used for right hand page of an open book marked by odd number?
(a) Recto (b) Octavo
(c) Half page (d) Quarto

849. What do you call a number of volumes related to one another and issued in sequence?
(a) Serials (b) Series (c) Title (d) Volumes

850. What term is given to the periodicity of a periodical issued twice in a year?
(a) Bi-Annual (b) Bieannual (c) Quarterly

851. What term is given to the periodicity of a periodical issued once in every two years?
(a) Bieannual (b) Bi-Annual (c) Quarterly

852. Which library periodical was first published in India in 1910-1913?
(a) *Library Journal* (b) *Library Printer*
(c) *Library Miscellany*

853. What is the full name of ABGILA?
(a) Annals, Bulletin and Granthalaya of Indian Library Association
(b) Annual Bulletin of Granthalaya of ILA
(c) Annals and Bulletin and Granthalaya of Indian Library Association

854. When was ABGILA started with Dr. S.R. Ranganathan as first editor?

(a) 1948 (b) 1949 (c) 1950

855. Which library periodical was first published in 1930 and edited by F. Mnubrary Volte?

(a) *Indian Librarian* (b) *Modern Librarian*
(c) *Library Herald*

856. Who published Index India in 1967?

(a) Delhi University (b) Rajasthan University
(c) Jodhpur University

857. When was *Book Review Digest* first published from New York by H.W. Wilson & Co.?

(a) 1903 (b) 1904 (c) 1905

858. Which journal was founded by J.D. Brown in 1898?

(a) *Library Herald* (b) *Library Trend*
(c) *Library World*

859. Who is the publisher of Ulritch's *International Periodical Directory*?

(a) W.H. Wilson, New York
(b) H.W. Wilson, London
(c) Bowker Co., New York

860. Which journal is published by Longman Group from Halow (Essex) since 1931 edited by Keesings?

(a) *Harlow Contemporary Archives*
(b) *Thomas Contemporary Archives*
(c) *Keesings Contemporary Archives*

861. When did the *Facts on File,* an international digest in English, start publishing?

(a) 1937 (b) 1938 (c) 1940

862. Which are two major newspaper indexes which forward news published in English?

(a) The Herald Times / World News Index, New York
(b) The Times Index / New York Times Index, New York

(c) The Times Index Reading (1790) & The New York Times Index (1851)

863. Which periodical index provides an index for U.N. Documents?

(a) UNINDEX (b) UNDOC (c) UNDEX

864. Which index is being published by Delhi Library Association since 1968?

(a) PRESS INDEX (b) DLA INDEX
(c) Indian Press Index

865. Who is the publisher of *Library & Information Science Abstracts* (1950)?

(a) LA (b) ALA (c) ILA

866. Indicate the publisher of *Press in India*:

(a) NSDOC, New Delhi
(b) Jain News Agency, New Delhi
(c) Registrar of Newspapers, New Delhi

867. What is new name of the periodical *Library Science with Slant to Documentation & Information Science* published from Bangalore?

(a) *SRELS Journal of Information Management*
(b) *Journal of Information Management*
(c) *Information Science and Technology*

868. Which journal on library science is published by Graduate School of Library Science of University of Texas at Austine?

(a) *Journal of Library Science (JLS)*
(b) *Journal of Library and Documentation (JLD)*
(c) *Journal of Library History (JLH)*

869. The Library Science Deptt. of which University is publishing 'Journal of American Society of Information Science' (JASIS)?

(a) Texas University (b) Drexel University
(c) Peninsula University

870. Which is the National Agency of ISBN in India?
   (a) Raja Ram Mohan Roy National Education Resource Centre
   (b) Parliament Library, New Delhi
   (c) Good Office Committee, New Delhi

871. Which is a monthly reviewing journal published by H.W. Wilson & Co. since 1905?
   (a) *Review Digest* (b) *Book Review Digest*
   (c) *Book Review Index*

872. Which Book Index is published by H.W. Wilson & Co., New York since 1928?
   (a) World Book Index
   (b) Cumulative Book Index
   (c) Cumulative Index

873. Who established Maharaja Public Library at Jaipur in 1866?
   (a) Maharaja Sawai Raja of Jaipur
   (b) Maharaja Sawai Madho Singh
   (c) Maharaja Sawai Ram Singh II

874. Who is publishing *Indian Psychological Abstract* since 1972 (Bi-monthly)?
   (a) CSIR (b) ICAR (c) ICSSR

875. Which mechanical system of retrieval of Text was initiated in 1961 which became operational on an IBM computer in 1964?
   (a) MARC-I system (b) MARC-II system
   (c) SMART system

876. Which book supports a teaching programme?
   (a) General book (b) Textbook (c) Serials

877. Which book gives general expositions of the subject in a general way?
   (a) Reference book (b) Periodicals
   (c) General book

878. Which books are consulted for reference or referred for a definite piece of information?
(a) Textbooks (b) General books
(c) Reference books

879. Which sources of information are conceptual, empirical and provide procedural information?
(a) Secondary sources (b) Primary sources
(c) Bibliographical sources

880. In which kind of information sources, research reports, proceedings and patents are considered?
(a) Secondary sources (b) Tertiary sources
(c) Primary sources

881. Do all secondary sources depend on primary sources?
(a) Yes (b) No

882. In which category of information sources are the encyclopedia, handbooks, manuals and indexing of periodicals considered?
(a) Secondary sources (b) Primary sources
(c) Tertiary sources

883. Do you agree that secondary sources have no existence of their own?
(a) Yes (b) No

884. In which category of information sources is the *Bibliography of Bibliographies* considered?
(a) Secondary sources (b) Tertiary sources
(c) Primary sources

885. Who formulated 91 rules for British Museum Library?
(a) C.A. Cutter (b) Panizzi (c) Paul Otlet

886. Which book was written by Paul Otlet, published in 1934?
(a) *Traite de Documentation*
(b) *A Book on Documentation*
(c) *Documentation Traite*

887. Which place is the headquarter of FID?
(a) Brussels (b) Paris (c) Hague

888. What is the first name of *British Books in Print*, which was changed later?
(a) *Catalogue of Current Literature*
(b) *Reference Catalogue of Current Literature*
(c) *British Reference Manual*
(d) *British Reference Books in Print*

889. Which classification scheme is used in 'Aslib book list', which started publication in 1935 in London?
(a) UDC (b) IDC
(c) CC (d) K.C. (Knowledge Classification)

890. What is frequency of publication of British National Bibliography?
(a) Annual (b) Quarterly
(c) Bi-annual (d) Weekly

891. What is frequency of publication of "British Books in Print"?
(a) Bi-annual (b) Weekly
(c) Quarterly (d) Annual

892. What is frequency of publication of "Books in Print"?
(a) Annual (b) Bi-annual
(c) Weekly (d) Quarterly

893. When did *Books in Print* first started its publication?
(a) 1946 (b) 1947 (c) 1948 (d) 1949

894. Which world list of scientific books in English language is published by H.W. Wilson, New York?
(a) *Books Review Digest*
(b) *Books in Print*
(c) *Publisher's Weekly*
(d) *Cumulative Book Index*

895. For whom is the term "Granthalai" used?
(a) Dy. Librarian (b) Librarian
(c) Chief Librarian

896. What name (term) is given to dictionary-making?
   (a) Directory (b) Lexicography
   (c) Lexigraphy
897. Which phrase was first used by Margaret Hutchins in her book introduction Reference Work published in 1943?
   (a) Reference Service (b) Reference Interview
   (c) Reference Work
898. Identify the book which was compiled by N.N. Gidwani and published in 1974 by Saraswati Prakashan, Jaipur?
   (a) *Reference Work on India*
   (b) *Reference Sources of India*
   (c) *A Guide to Reference Material in India*
899. How many parts are there in Asian Recorder?
   (a) Two (b) Three (c) Four
900. Who published 'Dictionary of National Biography'?
   (a) University Press, London
   (b) Macmillan & Co., London
   (c) Wilson & Co., London
901. Which encyclopedia consists of three parts—macropaedia, micropaedia and propaedia?
   (a) *Encyclopaedia Americana*
   (b) *Encyclopaedia Britannica*
   (c) *Crompton's Encyclopaedia*
902. Who is publishing *Documentation Fortnightly* since 1975?
   (a) Nehru Museum Library
   (b) Parliament Library of India
   (c) Delhi Library Association
903. Who compiled and edited the *Linguistic Survey of India* (1903-28)
   (a) N.K. Grierson (b) R.M. Robertson
   (c) G.A. Grierson

904. How many parts *Statesman's Year Book* published by Macmillan, London contains?

(a) 2 Parts (b) 3 Parts (c) 4 Parts

905. Which edition of *ALA Glossary of Library Terms* was edited by Heat Young in 1982?

(a) First edition (b) Second edition
(c) Third edition

906. Which biography was published by Sahitya Academy, New Delhi in 1985?

(a) *Who's Who in India*

(b) *Who's Who in Indians*

(c) *Who's Who of Indian Writers*

907. Which Gazetteer was published for the first time in India in 1881?

(a) *Ancient India Gazetteer* (b) *Gazetteer of India*
(c) *Imperial Gazetteer of India*

908. Which is the largest Gazetteer of the world published from London?

(a) *The World Gazetteer* (b) *The Times Index*
(c) *The World Index*

909. With which source of information the *INFA Press and Advertisers Year Book* deals?

(a) Indian publishers

(b) Indian press and publishers

(c) Indian press and advertisers

910. Which news bulletin is published by Association of Indian Universities to give current information of doctoral dissertations of Indian Universities?

(a) *Dissertations News* (b) *University News*
(c) *University News of India*

911. Which is the famous Almanack published from London?

(a) *Almanack World* (b) *World Almanack*
(c) *Whitaker's Almanacks*

912. Who is the publisher of *International Who's Who*?
   (a) Wilson, New York (b) Europa, London
   (c) Macmillan, London

913. Which bulletin was published by UNESCO in the field of libraries?
   (a) *Bulletin of Libraries*
   (b) *UNESCO Bulletin for Library Science*
   (c) *UNESCO Bulletin for Libraries*

914. Which handbook is being published by Association of Commonwealth Universities since 1914?
   (a) *University Handbook*
   (b) *Commonwealth University Handbook*
   (c) *Commonwealth University Yearbook*

915. Who published *Directory of Libraries* in Delhi in 1973?
   (a) Sterling, New Delhi
   (b) Metropolitan Book Co., New Delhi
   (c) Concept Publishing House, New Delhi

916. Which is important in print service covering the African countries?
   (a) African Book Publishing Record
   (b) African Publishing in Print Service
   (c) African Book in Print Record

917. When did Indian National Bibliography first start its publication?
   (a) 1956 (b) 1957 (c) 1958 (d) 1959

918. What is frequency of publication of Indian National Bibliography?
   (a) Weekly (b) Annual
   (c) Quarterly (d) Bi-annual

919. Which body/institution is publishing Indian National Bibliography?
   (a) Central Reference Library, Delhi
   (b) Delhi Public Library

(c) Central Reference Library, National Library
(d) Canmera Library

920. When was Indian Standard Institute established?
(a) 1945 (b) 1946 (c) 1947 (d) 1948

921. In which year was Hussain Memorial Library established in New Delhi?
(a) Feb. 6, 1972 (b) Feb. 6, 1973
(c) Aug. 15, 1972 (d) Aug. 15, 1973

922. What is full form of ISBD?
(a) Indian Standard Bibliographic Description
(b) International Standard Bibliographic Description
(c) International Standard Book Distribution
(d) Indian Standard Book Description

923. When was National Commission on Libraries and Information Science, under PL-345 set up in U.S.A.?
(a) July 20, 1970 (b) July 20, 1971
(c) Oct. 20, 1971 (d) Oct. 21, 1971

924. When was National Book Trust established in India?
(a) 1956 (b) 1957 (c) 1958 (d) 1959

LIBRARY MANAGEMENT

925. Who produced first successful Roman type in 1470?
(a) W. Humphrey (b) John Bradman
(c) Nicholas Jenson

926. Identify the animal whose skin is used for Morocco leather:
(a) Cow skin (b) Goat skin
(c) Neither (a) nor (b)

927. What term is used for a blank leaf at the beginning or end of book?
(a) Plane leaf (b) Blank leaf (c) Fly leaf

928. What term is used for heavy faced type?
(a) Bold face type (b) Bold type
(c) Heavy bold face

929. What type of bookbinding is called library bound?
(a) Soft bound (b) Paperback bound
(c) Hard bound

930. What term is applied to reproductions made by photographic or lithographic process?
(a) Colophon (b) Facsimile (c) Chronogram

931. During 7th to 12th century palm leaves were used as writing material as:
(a) Bhojpatra (b) Papyrus (c) Neither of them

932. Ivory was used as writing material by:
(a) Engraving (b) Writing (c) Neither of them

933. In pre-historical age, when man first learned to hunt animals, he started the use of skin for:
(a) Writing (b) Spinning (c) Both of them

934. Which library of Baghdad had a collection of clay tablets?
(a) Akur Library (b) Akkad Library
(c) Augad Library

935. In which area librarians used some type of chemicals in 993 A.D. to control the attack of termites?
(a) Ibn Ardoshir (Bagdac)
(b) Thebes and Memphis
(c) None of them

936. What was the method adopted for preservation of library collection to prevent from humidity and insects by Roman Emperor Fedrick-II in 1221 A.D.?
(a) Wooden boxes (b) Paper boxes
(c) Cardboard boxes

937. Which newspaper was printed on rag paper in 1927?
(a) *New York Times* (b) *London Times*
(c) *Hindustan Times*

938. In which year paper replaced Papyrus in Egypt?
(a) 910 A.D. (b) 950 A.D. (c) 1000 A.D.

939. In which year Ronair Reaumur in Germany first thought of using wood for manufacturing paper?

(a) 1700 (b) 1719 (c) 1729

940. In which country Mathias Koope first started manufacturing paper using straw and hay material?

(a) U.S.A. (b) U.K. (c) India

941. Who invented first machine of printing for continuous printing?

(a) Nicholas Louis Robert (b) Mathias Koope
(c) George Allen

942. Who invented improved cylinder machine in 1809?

(a) John Dickinson (b) John Gamble
(c) Bryan Donkin

943. Who suggested minimum standards for non-coated chemical wood paper which can be used for printing for the first time?

(a) W.J. Barrow (b) William James
(c) Cookworthy

944. Who invented Smith method of deacidification in 1970?

(a) Richard D. Smith (b) John Smith
(c) Smithsonian Institute

945. Who invented Barrow method patented in 1972 for deacidification?

(a) W.P. Barrow (b) G.P. Barrow (c) W.J. Barrow

946. Who invented William and Kelley method patented in 1976?

(a) John C. William and George V. Kelley Jr.

(b) John R. William and John Kelley

(c) John William and George V. Kelley Jr.

947. Which writing material was used in ancient Egypt, derived from a species of a road plentiful in Nile Delta?

(a) Parchment (b) Papyrus
(c) Neither (a) nor (b)

948. With which term the 12 points type size was called?
(a) Octava (b) Pica (c) Stug

949. When was the first printing press established in India?
(a) 1955 (b) 1956 (c) 1957

950. What do you call the 'types' casted by a machine?
(a) Pantograph (b) Autograph
(c) Machinegraph (d) Typograph

951. Which is a mutual antipathy of water and grease in printing?
(a) Photography (b) Composigraphy
(c) Lithography (d) Typography

952. Which type of composition involves two parts?
(a) Composing machine/Keyboard machine
(b) Composing machine/Casting machine
(c) Keyboard machine/Casting machine

953. Which is a birthplace of Conard Von Gesner?
(a) Paris (b) Melbourne
(c) Zurich (d) Sydney

954. When Conard Von Gesner started publishing *Bibliotica Universalis* a Catalogue of Greek?
(a) 1543 (b) 1545 (c) 1546 (d) 1550

955. Who was the physician, who became the secretary of Smithsonian Institute in 1846?
(a) Charles C. Jewett (b) Joseph Henry
(c) Fremant Rider

956. Who suggested Stereotype catalogues by separate title to ALA in 1850?
(a) Joseph Henry (b) C.A. Cutter
(c) Charles C. Jewett

957. Which International Catalogue was published in 1901 in 22 volumes in U.K.
(a) *International Catalogue of Scientific Literature*
(b) *International Catalogue of English Literature*
(c) *World Catalogue of Scientific Literature*

958. Who organised the conference in 1950 on Improvement of Bibliographical services?

(a) IFLA (b) FID (c) UNESCO (d) ASLIB

959. In which year FID was known with the name of 'Federation of National and International Group of Documentation'?

(a) 1922 (b) 1924 (c) 1940 (d) 1946

960. In which year UNESCO formed the International Committee for Intellectual Cooperation (IICL)?

(a) 1925 (b) 1927 (c) 1929

961. In which year the name IFLA was adopted in conference held at Stockholm?

(a) 1928 (b) 1930 (c) 1931 (d) 1932

962. In which meeting of cataloguing experts (IMCE) the ISBD project was workout, held in Copenhagen?

(a) 1968 (b) 1969 (c) 1970 (d) 1971

963. Which was the ambitious programme of IFLA in the field of bibliography?

(a) Bibliographical Project (BP)

(b) Bibliographical Control Programme (BCP)

(c) Universal Bibliographical Control (UBC)

964. How many countries were members of IFLA in 1994?

(a) 122 (b) 125 (c) 130 (d) 135

965. Which are four core programmes undertaken by IFLA in 1992-1997?

(a) UAP, UBCIM, PAC, UDT (b) UAP, PAC, UDT

(c) UCBIM, PAC, UDT

(d) UBCIM, UBC, PAC, UDT

966. Who organised International Conference on Science Abstract at Paris in June 1949?

(a) FID (b) IFLA (c) UNESCO

967. Which conference was organised by UNESCO in Paris in Nov. 1950?
   (a) International Conference on the Improvement of Bibliographical Services
   (b) International Conference on Bibliographical Control
   (c) International Conference on Establishment of Documentation Centres

968. In which years three National Documentation Centres of Mexico, India, Cairo were established with the help of UNESCO, respectively?
   (a) 1948, 1950, 1952 (b) 1950, 1952, 1954
   (c) 1951, 1953, 1955

969. Who published and sponsored 'World Fisheries Abstract' in 1950?
   (a) UNESCO (b) ILO (c) FAO

970. Who published and sponsored the International Occupational Safety and Health Services Abstract?
   (a) ILO (b) FID (c) UNESCO

971. Who is publishing 'Nuclear Science Abstract'?
   (a) INIS (b) IFLA (c) UNESCO

972. When was the first free public library started in Washington?
   (a) 1847 (b) 1848 (c) 1849 (d) 1850

973. When was the Malicious Damage Act passed in U.K.?
   (a) 1859 (b) 1860 (c) 1861

974. When was the report submitted by Kenyon Committee in U.K.?
   (a) 1925 (b) 1926 (c) 1927

975. Which committee submitted its report on Public Library System in 1942 in U.K.?
   (a) Kenyon Committee (b) Robert Committee
   (c) McColvin Committee

976. What post was Mr. McColvin holding in Library Association during 1940-42?
    (a) Secretary (b) President
    (c) Honorary Secretary

977. Which committee presented its report to the Parliament in Feb. 1959 in U.K.?
    (a) McColvin Committee (b) Robert Committee
    (c) Kenyon Committee

978. When was Public Libraries and Museum Act passed and came in operation respectively in U.K.?
    (a) July 1964/April 1965
    (b) June 1964/March 1965
    (c) July 1964/May 1965

979. When was the Library of Congress established?
    (a) 1878 (b) 1880 (c) 1882 (d) 1884

980. Who was the Librarian of Library of Congress during 1899-1939?
    (a) Melvil Dewey (b) Herbert Putnam
    (c) Berwick Sayers

981. When was the Public Library Catalogue of LC published?
    (a) 1899 (b) 1900 (c) 1901

982. Who used the term 'Selective Dissemination of Information' for the first time in 1959?
    (a) Lubuskey (b) Peter Luhn
    (c) Herbert Putnam

983. Who started first library school in India in 1911 in Baroda?
    (a) A.D. Dickinson (b) W.A. Border
    (c) S.R. Ranganathan

984. When was the first library school in Punjab University started by A.D. Dickinson?
    (a) 1910 (b) 1912 (c) 1915

985. Who represented UNESCO to India in 1972 on short-term Mission to establish NISSAT?
(a) F.N. Nithers (b) Peter Laazar
(c) S.R. Ranganathan

986. When was NISSAT established?
(a) March, 1979 (b) April, 1979 (c) April, 1980

987. Where is VINITY situated?
(a) Budapest (b) Moscow (c) Leningrad

988. When was VINITY established?
(a) 1950 (b) 1951 (c) 1952

989. Who is sponsoring body of Social Science Documentation Centre?
(a) ISI (b) INSDOC (c) ICSSR

990. When was Social Science Documentation Centre established in Delhi?
(a) 1967 (b) 1968 (c) 1969

991. Who devised Sears' list of subject headings?
(a) H.E. Bliss (b) M.E. Sears
(c) Joseph Miller

992. Which is the last edition in use of Sears' list of subject headings?
(a) 15th edition (b) 16th edition
(c) 17th edition (d) 18th edition

993. Who is the editor of 17th edition of Sears' list of subject headings?
(a) Carolina Reyers (b) Martha T. Mooney
(c) Joseph Miller

994. What is full form of BT used in Sears list of subject headings?
(a) Big Term (b) Behind Term
(c) Broad Term

995. What is full form of NT used in Sears list of subject headings?
   (a) Near Term (b) Nearer Term
   (c) Narrower Term

996. What is full form of RT used in Sears list of subject headings?
   (a) Rear Term (b) Related Term
   (c) Reach Term

997. Which directing word is used in bold letters in Sears list of subject headings?
   (a) PUT (b) SELECT (c) USE

998. Which index was prepared by Eloise Rue in 1938?
   (a) Subject Index to Users
   (b) Subject Index to Readers
   (c) A Subject Index to Americans

999. When was the International Index started by Poole System?
   (a) 1910 (b) 1911 (c) 1912 (d) 1913

1000. Which is the important catalogue/index for pamphlets which began in 1952?
   (a) File Service Catalogue
   (b) Vertical File Service Catalogue
   (c) Vertical File Service Index

1001. Which book is written by Edwin L. Shuman published by Houghton in 1910?
   (a) *Book Judgment* (b) *Judge Your Book*
   (c) *How to Judge a Book*

1002. Is there a separate index for *British Books in Print*?
   (a) Yes (b) No

1003. How many digits ISBN contains?
   (a) 7 digits (b) 8 digits (c) 9 digits (d) 10 digits

1004. When did ISBN number come into use?
   (a) 1968 (b) 1969 (c) 1970

1005. Which system gives full liberty to the reader to browse amongst books without any barrier?

(a) Closed Access System (b) Open Access System
(c) Neither of above

1006. Which is the key to library resources which helps in finding a reader for every book?

(a) Library catalogue (b) A Bibliography
(c) INB

1007. Which term is used for the art of getting things done through and with people in formally organised group, quoted by Harald Coontz?

(a) Organisation (b) Management
(c) Controlling

1008. Who used the word PODSCORB to describe the functions of management?

(a) Joseph Massie (b) Luther Gulick
(c) C.W. Wilson

1009. Who listed fourteen principles of Management?

(a) Mary Parker Follett (b) Henri Fayal
(c) Luther Gulick

1010. Which study is the science of eliminating wasteful resulting from using unnecessary, ill-directed and inefficient motions, examined by Frank Gilbert?

(a) Time study (b) Motion Study
(c) Method study

1011. Which is an independent committee which is delegated powers by the competent authority?

(a) Advisory Committee

(b) Executive Committee

(c) Standing Committee

1012. Who developed zero-based Budgeting (ZBB)?

(a) Peter Phyor (b) S. Setharan
(c) A. Neelameghan

1013. In which charging system a piece of wood or cardboard about equal to the size of an ordinary book is used?
(a) Ledger System (b) Dummy System
(c) Indicator System

1014. Who introduced photographic charging system?
(a) Ralph R. Show
(b) Miss Nina E. Browne
(c) John Cotton Dana

1015. How many students were in first school of library science established by Melvil Dewey in 1887?
(a) 18 (b) 20 (c) 21

1016. Which postgraduate course was started in Madras University in 1937?
(a) Diploma Course
(b) Post Graduate Diploma Course
(c) Bachelor Course

1017. Who was awarded Ph.D. degree in Library Science as first person in India?
(a) D.B. Krishna Rao
(b) S.R. Ranganathan
(c) Jagdish Saran Sharma

1018. Which body of Great Britain is offering training of librarianship since 1898?
(a) LA (b) ALA (c) British Museum

1019. What degree or certificate is being awarded by the Library Association of Great Britain?
(a) (FLA) Fellowship of the LA
(b) Fellowship of Librarianship
(c) Certificate in Librarianship

1020. Which University of India is running the B.Lib. Sc. Course for Women only?
(a) Bombay University (b) Punjab University
(c) SNDT University

1021. When was the Public Library Act passed in Great Britain?

(a) 1948 (b) 1949 (c) 1950

1022. Who was the first Indian Linguist who became the National Librarian in 1907-10?

(a) B.S. Kesavan (b) Harinath De
(c) S.R. Ranganathan

1023. Who appointed Parry Committee in 1967 in Great Britain?

(a) UGC, U.K. (b) LA, U.K.
(c) British Govt.

1024. Which Public Library Bill was drafted by Kumar Murindra Deb Rai?

(a) Vishwa-Bharti Public Library Bill
(b) Bengal Public Library Act
(c) Bihar Public Library Act

1025. Which Library Committee was headed by K.P. Sinha in 1957?

(a) Public Library Committee
(b) Sinha Committee for Libraries
(c) Advisory Committee for Libraries

1026. When was NASSADOC established?

(a) 1969 (b) 1970 (c) 1971

1027. Who Published *Indian Press Index* in 1968?

(a) Indian Library Association
(b) Delhi Library Association
(c) INSDOC

1028. Which is the Fourth Law of Library Science enunciated by S.R. Ranganathan?

(a) Books are for use
(b) Library is a growing organism
(c) Save the time of the reader

1029. What is the name of the record in which books are entered when withdrawn or written off?

(a) Written off register

(b) Withdrawal register

(c) Lost book register

1030. What do we call the area or part of a library where books are kept or arranged for service?

(a) Store room (b) Collection room

(c) Stack room

1031. Who stressed for open access system for the first time?

(a) James Duff Brown (b) S.R. Ranganathan

(c) J.S. Mill

1032. What term is used for the passageway between two parallel book racks?

(a) Way (b) Aisle (c) Bay

1033. Which term devotes the statistical study of Library Science and Service and was coined by S.R. Ranganathan?

(a) Libramacy (b) Librametry

(c) Libra

1034. Which charging system was devised by Miss Nina E. Browne in 1895?

(a) Network charging system

(b) Browne charging system

(c) Ledger system

1035. Which charging system was first introduced by Public Library of Network of New Jersey State (U.S.A.) in 1900?

(a) Ledger System

(b) Newark charging system

(c) Brown charging system

1036. Who introduced colour charging system in 1948-49 in Detroit (U.S.A.)?

(a) Ninc E. Browne (b) C.A. Cutter

(c) Walter H. Kaister

1037. Who introduced Network charging system?
   (a) John Cotton Dana (b) James Duff Brown
   (c) S.R. Ranganathan

1038. Which charging system was introduced by Gaylord Brothers in 1932?
   (a) Electricity operated charging system
   (b) Electricity charging system
   (c) Mechanical operated charging system

1039. Which Kardex Visible record for periodical was invented by Ramington Rand (U.S.A.)?
   (a) System Kardex (b) Serial Kardex
   (c) Robot Kardex

1040. What is other name for 'Dictaphone charging system'?
   (a) Audio charging system
   (b) Automatic charging system
   (c) Dicta-charging system

1041. Which charging system was developed by Ralph A. Ulveling in 1929?
   (a) Detroit self-charging system
   (b) Dekker self-charging system
   (c) Ralph charging system

1042. What is the name given by S.R. Ranganathan for Book-Mobile?
   (a) Libra-drive (b) Libra chine
   (c) Libra-mob.

1043. Which register records the holdings of books and journals in a library?
   (a) Stock register (b) Periodical register
   (c) Order register (d) Accession register

LIBRARY & SOCIETY

1044. Who introduced 'Three card system' for periodicals?
   (a) Sayers (b) C.A. Cutter
   (c) S.R. Ranganathan

1045. Who was the Chairman of "Working Group of the Planning Commission on Modernisation of Library Services and Information"?

(a) Mr. Seshagiri (b) Mr. B.S. Kesavan
(c) Mr. Girja Kumar

1046. In which year Raja Ram Mohan Roy Library Foundation was established by Central Government?

(a) 1971 (b) 1972 (c) 1973

1047. The logical steps involved in scientific investigation are:

(a) Identification of the problem
(b) Formulation of the hypothesis
(c) Collection of data
(d) All the above

1048. Among the following which has been considered as a library of national importance?

(a) Saraswati Mahal Library
(b) Delhi Public Library
(c) Khuda Baksh Oriental Library
(d) The Rampur Raza Library

1049. The term 'lexicography' is associated with:

(a) Compilation of Encyclopedia
(b) Compilation of Handbooks
(c) Compilation of Dictionaries
(d) None of the above

1050. Under whose leadership Indian Library Association started library training in 1933?

(a) K.M. Asadullah (b) S.R. Ranganathan
(c) B.S. Kesavan (d) D.R. Kalia

1051. Which library training was first started in Delhi University under the leadership of Dr. S.R. Ranganathan in 1947?

(a) Degree Course (b) M.A. in Library Science
(c) Diploma Course (d) Certificate Course

1052. When did S.R. Ranganathan become the librarian of Madras University?

(a) Jan. 1924 (b) Feb. 1924 (c) March 1924

1053. When was the British Library established in London?

(a) 1972 (b) 1973 (c) 1974

1054. When Dr. S.R. Ranganathan died?

(a) Sept. 24, 1972 (b) Sept. 25, 1972
(c) Sept. 27, 1972

1055. Who founded London Library on May 3, 1841?

(a) Thomas Carlyle (b) Thomas Hardy
(c) James Carlyle

1056. Who inaugurated DRTC Bangalore on Aug. 18, 1962?

(a) G.B. Pant (b) C.D. Deshmukh
(c) Smt. Indira Gandhi

1057. Who inaugurated Delhi Public Library on Oct. 27, 1951?

(a) Smt. Indira Gandhi (b) Pt. Jawaharlal Nehru
(c) Dr. S. Radhakrishnan

1058. When was UNESCO established?

(a) Nov. 2, 1946 (b) Nov. 3, 1946
(c) Nov. 4, 1946

1059. Who was first editor of Library Association Record started in 1899?

(a) Henry Guppy (b) Henry James
(c) Henry Thomson

1060. In which language the work 'microform' has literary meaning 'small card'?

(a) German (b) Italian (c) French

1061. Which committee in India was formed to establish uniform terms of book supply to libraries and recommend the conversion rates of rupee in foreign currency from time to time?

(a) Publishers Committee

(b) University Grant Committee

(c) Good Office Committee

1062. Which association of India formulated rules and created 'Inter-Library Loan Code'?

(a) ILA (b) IASLIC (c) DRTC

1063. Who is publishing *Food Technology Abstracts* Monthly in India?

(a) NICFOS (b) ICRISET (c) ICAR

1064. Who was the Chairman of Ray Committee of INSDOC of 1967?

(a) Siddharth Shankar Ray (b) Kamalendu Ray
(c) Nihar Ranjan Ray

1065. Who formed 'Atkinson Committee' of Great Britain in 1976 to deal with the space problems of University Libraries?

(a) Govt. of Great Britain (b) British Library
(c) UGC of Great Britain

1066. Who was founder President of Chhattisgarh Library Association?

(a) R.S. Tiwari (b) Dr. C.K. Sharma
(c) R.S. Dwivedi

1067. Who is the publisher of *Who's Who: An Annual Bibliographical Dictionary,* started in 1949?

(a) Adam and Charles, London

(b) Wilson & Co., London

(c) Macmillan & Co., London

1068. When was the National Library for Visually Handicapped established in Dehradun?

(a) 1961 (b) 1962 (c) 1963

1069. How many National Libraries are there in Italy?

(a) Five (b) Six (c) Seven (d) Eight

1070. Who was the founder editor of *Indian Librarian,* started in 1946?

(a) R.N. Bhati (b) S.R. Bhatia
(c) R.K. Bansal

1071. What was the pseudonym used by S.R. Ranganathan for writing articles?

(a) Ranga (b) Libra (c) Professor R.

1072. In which year S. Bashiruddin was awarded 'Padmashri' by Govt. of India?

(a) 1975 (b) 1976 (c) 1978

1073. Who was the founder president of Madras Library Association?

(a) K.V. Krishnaswami Aiyer

(b) S.R. Ranganathan

(c) D.B. Rao

1074. Who was the compiler of National Biographical Dictionary of India published in 1972 by Sterling?

(a) S.R. Bhatia (b) Jagdish Saran Sharma
(c) P.N. Kaula

1075. Which emperor appointed Amir Khusro as Librarian of Imperial Library at Delhi?

(a) Emperor Akbar (b) Jalaluddin Khilji
(c) Allauddin Khilji

1076. When is the National Library week of India celebrated?

(a) Nov. 8-14 every year (b) Nov. 14-20 every year
(c) Nov. 10-17 every year

1077. Who publishes *Library Trends*?

(a) University of California (b) University of Illinois
(c) University of Kansas

1078. Who devised the selection system of post coordinate indexing?

(a) G. Gardner (b) G. Cordonnier (c) G. Fentum

1079. Which fund awards Kaula Gold Medal, Ranganathan Kaula Award and Kaula Annual Prize?

(a) Sarada Ranganathan Endowment for Lib. Sc.

(b) Prof. Kaula Endowment for Lib. & Inf. Science

(c) Kaula Ranganathan Endowment for Lib. & Inf. Science

1080. Who coined the term pre-netal classification?
(a) C.A. Cutter (b) H.E. Bliss
(c) S.R. Ranganathan

1081. Who was Member Secretary of the working group on modernization of Library and Information Science appointed by Planning Commission?
(a) P.N. Kaula (b) P.B. Mangla
(c) J.L. Sardhana

1082. When was the first International Congress on Archivists and Librarians held in Brussels?
(a) 1905 (b) 1910 (c) 1915

1083. Who was the first wife of S.R. Ranganathan?
(a) Smt. Sarada (b) Smt. Rukmini
(c) Smt. Anupama

1084. What term you give to books printed before 1501 AD?
(a) Incunabula (b) Manuscripts
(c) Rare Books

1085. What is old name of World Atlas published by John Bartholomew?
(a) *Edinburgh World Atlas* (b) *Classic World Atlas*
(c) *New World Atlas*

1086. What is the old name of *Information Science Abstract* published from U.S.A.?
(a) *Science Abstract* (b) *Documentation Abstract*
(c) *Documentation Science Abstract*

1087. What is old term of superimposition device?
(a) Auto device (b) Auto-bias device
(c) Auto super device

1088. With which name was Hardayal Municipal Library, Delhi known previously?
(a) Hardinge Library
(b) Hardinge Municipal Library
(c) Delhi Hardinge Library

1089. What is the name of FID committee on classification theory founded in 1950?

(a) FID/CT (b) FID/TC (c) FID/CR

1090. With which name is the *Chamber's Technical Dictionary* known now?

(a) *Chambers Dictionary of Technology*

(b) *Chambers Dictionary of Science*

(c) *Chambers Dictionary of Science & Technology*

1091. Who developed the Saraswati Mahal Library at Tanjore during 1798-1833?

(a) Dr. Burnell (b) Nayak
(c) Maharaja Raja (d) Maharaja Sarfoji II

1092. Who was the founder of Adyar Library in 1879 on the bank of Adyar river?

(a) Dr. Gravelty (b) Lord Conmera
(c) Dr. Edger Thurston (d) Col. Henry Stedeolcott

1093. For what purpose Dr. S.R. Ranganathan donated Rs. one lakh out of his life's saving to Madras University?

(a) Development of University Library

(b) To start Library Science Course

(c) For a chair in Library Science

1094. When was National Book Trust inaugurated in India by Dr. C.D. Deshmukh as Chairman of the trust?

(a) Aug. 1, 1956 (b) Aug. 1, 1957
(c) Aug. 1, 1958 (d) Aug. 1, 1959

1095. Which University conferred D. Lit. to Dr. S.R. Ranganathan for meritorious works and service to library profession on March 7, 1948 by Lord Mountbatten, as Chancellor?

(a) Benaras Hindu University (b) Madras University
(c) Delhi University (d) Agra University

1096. When was 'Padmashri' awarded to Dr. S.R. Ranganathan?

(a) 1957 (b) 1958 (c) 1959 (d) 1960

1097. What is the date of birth of Melvil Dewey?

(a) Dec. 5, 1850 (b) Dec. 15, 1850

(c) Dec. 11, 1850

1098. Which type of numericals are used in Dewey Decimal Classification?

(a) Arabic (b) Indo-Arabic (c) Alphabets

1099. When did Dewey submit his first plan of classifying the book in his college?

(a) May 1, 1873 (b) May 8, 1973

(c) Aug. 8, 1973 (d) Aug. 8, 1974

1100. Which post Dewey accepted after leaving Amherst College?

(a) Editor, American Library Journal

(b) Editor, American Journal of Public Library

(c) Asstt. Editor, American Library Journal

1101. Which post Dewey held in American Library Association?

(a) Secretary, 1976-1890

(b) President 1890-1893

(c) Secretary & President Both

1102. When did Dewey marry Annie R. Godfrey?

(a) Sept. 10, 1875 (b) Oct. 19, 1876

(c) Oct. 19, 1877

1103. When was the Madras Public Library Act passed?

(a) 1947 (b) 1948 (c) 1949 (d) 1950

1104. Which library authority levies library cess in the form of surcharge on the property tax or house tax in Madras?

(a) Local Library Authority

(b) Regional Library Authority

(c) District Library Authority

(d) State Library Authority

1105. Who is the highest authority of FID?

(a) President (b) General Secretary (c) Chairman

1106. When did Dr. S.R. Ranganathan establish Sarda Ranganathan Endowment for Library Science, Bangalore?

(a) 1961 (b) 1966 (c) 1967

1107. Which law directs to follow display, exhibition of books, proper book selection and open access system?

(a) Second law (b) First law
(c) Third law (d) None of these

1108. Name the service which refers to the reference sources and personal approach?

(a) Circulation Service (b) Documentation service
(c) Enquiry service (d) Reference service

1109. Which three factors in a library are called Trinity?

(a) Building/documents/readers
(b) Document/readers/staff
(c) Periodicals/readers/staff

1110. Which is the perfect and adequate service, which provides door-to-door service?

(a) Communication service
(b) Library enquiry service
(c) Publicity service
(d) Mobile service

1111. Who was the invader who carried away the library holdings to Persia in 1739?

(a) Mohammed Shah (b) Mohd. Gauri
(c) Nadir Shah (d) Gul-Badan Begham

1112. Which are the four cardinal points of the spiral of scientific method of Dr. S.R. Ranganathan?

(a) Nadir/observation/hypothesis/zenith
(b) Nadir/ascendent/zenith/hypothesis
(c) Nadir/ascendent/zenith/descendent

1113. When was the Library of Congress, Washington established?

(a) April 24, 1800 (b) April 24, 1801
(c) April 24, 1802 (d) April 24, 1803

1114. Who was the first librarian of Library of Congress, U.S.A.?

(a) Patrick Maguder (b) Herbert Watterston
(c) John James Backley (d) Herbert Putnam

1115. In which year Union Government appointed an Advisory Committee for Libraries?

(a) 1955 (b) 1956 (c) 1957 (d) 1958

1116. Who was the Chairman of Advisory Committee for Libraries appointed by Union Government in 1957?

(a) Dr. S.R. Ranganathan (b) D.R. Kalia
(c) B.S. Kesavan (d) K.P. Sinha

1117. When was the Library Legislation (Edward Act) first implemented in Great Britain?

(a) 1949 (b) 1950 (c) 1951 (d) 1952

1118. When was the first Municipal free public library established in U.K.?

(a) 1947 (b) 1948 (c) 1949 (d) 1950

1119. Give in sequence the years in which Kenyon Report, McColvin report, and Robert Committee reports, U.K. were submitted?

(a) 1927, 1942, 1959 (b) 1942, 1959, 1927
(c) 1959, 1927, 1942

1120. Who founded the Asiatic Society of Bengal?

(a) Lord Curzon (b) Tipu Sultan
(c) Sir William Jones (d) Lord Conmera

1121. In which year was The Khuda Baksh Oriental Public Library established?

(a) 1876 (b) 1877 (c) 1878 (d) 1879

1122. What is full form of NISSAT, founded on 1977?
   (a) National Information Source of Science and Technology
   (b) National Infotech System for Science and Technology
   (c) National Information System for Science and Technology

1123. Who first drafted 'Model Library Act' in India?
   (a) Sri Kumar Munindra Dev Rai Maharaj
   (b) Mr. Gopalarao Ekbote
   (c) Dr. S.R. Ranganathan

1124. When did Madras Library Association start its first training course (C.Lib.)?
   (a) 1928 (b) 1929 (c) 1930 (d) 1931

1125. In which State did Panchayat Board first start libraries and reading rooms in the district in 1910?
   (a) Karnataka (b) Mysore
   (c) Tanjore (d) Andhra Pradesh

1126. In which year did The Tirumala Tirupati Devasthanams start S.V. Oriental Research Institute Library, Tirupati?
   (a) 1938 (b) 1939 (c) 1940 (d) 1941

1127. Who was a special invitee in IXth All India Library Conference, 1951 held at Indore?
   (a) Sayers (b) Frank M. Gardner
   (c) Lord Conmera

1128. In which year UNESCO launched 'Books for all' programme?
   (a) 1971 (b) 1972 (c) 1973 (d) 1974

1129. Which type of Director of Pubic Libraries has been provisioned in Tamil Nadu Public Library Act?
   (a) Non-professional (b) Professional
   (c) Semi professional (d) Govt. Officer

1130. In which year was *Webster's New International Dictionary* first published in Springfield?

(a) 1959 (b) 1960 (c) 1961 (d) 1962

1131. When was FID (Federation International de Documentation) established at Brussels?

(a) 1893 (b) 1894 (c) 1895 (d) 1896

1132. Which institution was founded by two pioneers, Henry La Fontaine and Paul Otlet in Brussels in 1895?

(a) IFLA (b) FID (c) VINITY (d) OECD

1133. When was IFLA (International Federation of Library Association) established at Geneva?

(a) 1927 (b) 1928 (c) 1929 (d) 1930

1134. When ISLIB (Association of Special Libraries and Information Bureau) was established at London?

(a) 1922 (b) 1923 (c) 1924 (d) 1925

1135. When did Formington Plan start in America?

(a) 1948 (b) 1949 (c) 1950 (d) 1951

1136. When was Press and Registration of Books Act (XXV) enacted in India?

(a) 1865 (b) 1866 (c) 1867 (d) 1868

1137. How many Indian languages are covered to prepare main entry, transliterated in Roman Script in Indian National Bibliography?

(a) 11 (b) 12 (c) 13 (d) 14

1138. Which is the State Central Library of Madras?

(a) Madras Public Library
(b) Municipal Library, Madras
(c) Town Hall Public Library, Madras
(d) Conmera Public Library, Madras

1139. When was Canadian Library Association formed?

(a) 1934 (b) 1935 (c) 1936 (d) 1937

1140. When did Benaras Hindu University start M.Lib. Sc. Course for the first time?

(a) 1963 (b) 1964 (c) 1965 (d) 1966

1141. When and where was Nehru Memorial Library established?

(a) May 12, 1968 in Allahabad

(b) May 27, 1969 in New Delhi

(c) Aug. 15, 1968 in Bombay

(d) Aug. 15, 1969 in Nagpur

1142. Where is Nehru Memorial Library situated in New Delhi?

(a) Tin Murti Bhavan

(b) Race Course

(c) Delhi Public Library Campus

(d) J.N.U. Campus

1143. Which library is known as Central Library of Mumbai?

(a) Asiatic Society Library (b) Town Hall Library

(c) Bombay Asiatic Society Library

1144. When was Mysore Public Library Act passed?

(a) 1965 (b) 1966 (c) 1967 (d) 1968

1145. With which name is the library of Delhi School of Economics (1949) known?

(a) Tata Library

(b) Central Library of Delhi School of Economics

(c) Ratan Tata Library

(d) Ratan Library

1146. When was Raja Ram Mohan Roy Library, Calcutta founded?

(a) May 29, 1971 (b) May 29, 1972

(c) Jan. 26, 1971 (d) Jan. 26, 1972

1147. When was Rampur Raza Library established?

(a) 1973 (b) 1974 (c) 1975 (d) 1976

1148. Which library first adopted CIP (Cataloguing in Publication Programme) in March 30, 1974?

(a) ALA (Amc. Lib. Asso.)

(b) LC (Lib. of Congress)

(c) Lib. Asso. London

(d) British Museum

1149. Who was the first Chairman of National Book Trust, New Delhi?

(a) K.S. Duggal (b) Dr. B.V. Keskar

(c) Dr. Karan Singh (d) Dr. Nihar Ranjan Ray

1150. Which course is being run by Delhi Library Association since 1955?

(a) B.Lib.Sc. (b) C.Lib.Sc.

(c) D.Lib.Sc. (d) M.Lib.Sc.

1151. When was the 'Bhatia Festschrift' presented to Mr. Sant Ram Bhatia, Editor, *Indian Librarian*?

(a) June 30, 1971 (b) June 30, 1972

(c) June 15, 1971 (d) June 15, 1972

1152. When was Kerala Library Association formed in Trivendrum?

(a) Oct. 10, 1971 (b) Oct. 11, 1971

(c) Oct. 12, 1971 (d) Oct. 13, 1971

1153. When was the Library Association of Afghanistan formed in Kabul?

(a) 1970 (b) 1971 (c) 1972 (d) 1973

1154. What is Birth year of Dr. S.R. Ranganathan?

(a) 1891 (b) 1892 (c) 1893 (d) 1894

1155. What was the previous name given in 1886 changed to Lala Hardayal Public Library?

(a) Hardinge Public Library

(b) Lord Curzon Public Library

(c) Delhi Municipal Library

(d) Municipal Library of Delhi

1156. Which is a Central Library where Buddhist manuscripts are being preserved?
   (a) Ladakh Buddha Vihar, New Delhi
   (b) Ladakh Vihar, New Delhi
   (c) Buddha Vihar Library, New Delhi
   (d) Ladakh Budha Library, New Delhi

1157. Which body launched TELESTAR, the first working communication satellite to orbit around earth, on July 18, 1962?
   (a) NASA (b) AT&T (c) COMSAT (d) INTELESAT

1158. Which Indian agency developed TELESTAR for operation in India?
   (a) NASA (b) COMSAT (c) INTELESAT

1159. Which satellite was lent to India by United States for the Satellite Instructional Television Experiment (SITE) programme?
   (a) ATS-6 Satellite (b) INSAT-I
   (c) INSAT-II

1160. When did the first Indian National Satellite (INSAT-IA) park in orbit about 36000 Kilometers above the equator, a new star in Indian Horizon?
   (a) 1981 (b) 1982 (c) 1983 (d) 1984

1161. Who was the first Indian Library of Free India's National Library, Calcutta?
   (a) S.R. Ranganathan (b) Dr. J.S. Sharma
   (c) P.N. Kaula (d) B.S. Kesavan

1162. Which is the important contribution of Shri B.S. Kesavan as Librarian of National Library, Calcutta?
   (a) *Indian Reference Manual*
   (b) *Indian National Bibliography*
   (c) *Selective List of Books*
   (d) *India's National Library Book List*

1163. Who was the author of *Who's Who in Librarianship* published in 1954?

(a) Robert L. Collins (b) Thomas Landau
(c) Margeret Mann (d) Paul Otlet

1164. Which is the important book of British Librarian Thomas Landau, published in 1961?

(a) *Handbook of Librarianship*
(b) *Primer of Librarianship*
(c) *Encyclopedia of Librarianship*
(d) *Librarian's Knowledge Book*

1165. Which post was held by Sir Anthony Panizzi in British Museum in 1856?

(a) Secretary (b) Editor
(c) Keeper (d) Chief Librarian

1166. Who is the first British Librarian who contributed to get the Public Library Act of 1919 passed?

(a) G.E. Roebock (b) R.R. Shaw
(c) Herbert Spencer (d) W.C.B. Sayers

1167. Which body in a University and College Library, discusses library problems and developments?

(a) Governing body
(b) Vice Chancellor/Principal
(c) Librarian
(d) Library Committee

1168. When was the International Symposium 'Library History Research in International Context' held in Walfenbuttel, Germany?

(a) April 1988 (b) March 1989 (c) April 1990

1169. Who understood a systematic overview of the situation in India during a five-week research tour in summer sponsored by American Institute of Indian studies?

(a) 1986 (b) 1987 (c) 1988

1170. Which is acronym of OPAC?
  (a) Online Public Access Catalogue
  (b) Online Process Access Catalogue
  (c) Online Public Acquisition Catalogue

1171. Which system is used in OPAC?
  (a) OCLC System
  (b) Lan Based Multimedia System
  (c) PLEXUS System

1172. When did OCLC create the first OPAC?
  (a) Jan. 1972 (b) Jan. 1974 (c) Jan. 1975

1173. When was America's Freedom of Information Act passed and assented by President Lyndon B. Johnson?
  (a) July 4, 1967 (b) July 4, 1968
  (c) July 4, 1969

1174. When was the 'Freedom of Information Act' passed in Australia?
  (a) 1981 (b) 1982 (c) 1983

1175. When was the 'Access to Information Act' passed in Canada?
  (a) 1981 (b) 1982 (c) 1983

1176. When was the movable type for book printing invented by Johnan Gutenberg?
  (a) 1451 (b) 1452 (c) 1453

1177. Which Information Bulletin provides information service to entrepreneurs and industry published in 3 parts from Hyderabad since 1973?
  (a) *Information Bulletin of SENDOC*
  (b) *Information SENDOC Bulletin*
  (c) *SENDOC Bulletin*

1178. Who (expert of UNESCO) recommended the establishment of NISSAT? (1977)
  (a) J. Clement Harrison (b) Adme Quane
  (c) Peter Lazer

1179. When was New National Policy of Education approved by Parliament?

(a) 1985 (b) 1986 (c) 1987

1180. When was Fourth International Conference of Adult Education convened by UNESCO?

(a) March 19-29, 1983 (b) March 19-29, 1984
(c) March 19-29, 1985

1181. Which Regional Conference, referred to as MINEDAP-V, met at Bangkok in 1985?

(a) Fourth (b) Fifth (c) Sixth

1182. District Libraries in Orissa started in:

(a) 1976 (b) 1977 (c) 1978

1183. Which library was established by Rai Bahadur Ishan in 1900 in Jaipur?

(a) Garden Library (b) Jaipur Library
(c) Pink City Library

1184. Who established Sanmati Pustakalaya in Rajasthan in 1920?

(a) Motilal Singhvi
(b) Sawai Madho Singh
(c) Sawai Ram Singh

1185. Which 'door to door free service' was provided by Sanmati Pustakalaya in Rajasthan?

(a) Dasti Pustak Sewa (b) Sasti Pustak Sewa
(c) Mufta Pustak Sewa

1186. When was Children Library established in Maharaja Public Library of Rajasthan?

(a) 1942 (b) 1943 (c) 1944

1187. When was State Public Library of Princely State Bharatpur established?

(a) 1901 (b) 1905 (c) 1907

1188. Which library was established by Maharaja of Kumbh in 1448 in Udaipur?

(a) Saraswati Bhandar Library

(b) Udaipur Central Library

(c) Kumbh Bhandar Library

1189. In which library, the three libraries—Rajgranthalaya (1628-52), Sajjanvani—Vilas Library (1874) Victoria Hall Library and Museum (1887) were amalgamated in Rajasthan?

(a) State Public Library (b) Motimahal Library
(c) Saraswati Bhavan Library

1190. When was the 'State Level Permanent Advisory Committee for Libraries' formed in Rajasthan?

(a) 1989 (b) 1991 (c) 1992

1191. Who was the Britisher who worked for the advancement of Telugu language and literature and centered in Madras in 1817 till death in London in 1884?

(a) C.P. Brown (b) James Hudson
(c) P.C. Brown

1192. C.P. Brown donated 5751 main scripts in different languages in 1845 to:

(a) Madras Central Library

(b) Madras Literary Society

(c) Madras Govt.

1193. Who prepared Draft Public Library Bill of Madhya Pradesh in 1948?

(a) Dr. G.D. Bhargava (b) Dr. C.S. Sharma
(c) Dr. S.R. Ranganathan

1194. Which 11 M library was first established in India?

(a) Ahmedabad (b) Lucknow
(c) Calcutta (d) Indore

1195. In which year was the ILA conference held at University of Indore?

(a) 1965 (b) 1967 (c) 1968

1196. Which Englishman was invited to review the Public Libraries of Madhya Bharat in 1952?

(a) A.D. Adinson (b) J.D. Brown
(c) Frank M. Gardner

1197. Who organised the Work Flow seminar "From Publisher to Reader: Work Flow in University and College Libraries", during March 4-7, 1959?

(a) UNESCO (b) UGC (c) ILA

1198. When "India Loan Educational Exchange Programme (PL 480)" came into existence to allow representative of 36 Universities and 52 Research Libraries of India to visit U.S.A. libraries?

(a) 1952-56 (b) 1955-61
(c) 1957-61

1199. When was Brown Memorial Trust formed in Cuddapah (India)?

(a) 1984 (b) 1986 (c) 1988

1200. In which conference was the first Model Library Act (drafted in 1930) presented for discussion during Dec. 26-30, 1930 in Benaras?

(a) Asian Educational Conference

(b) ILA Conference

(c) IASLIC Conference

1201. When did Mysore Public Library Act change its nomenclature to Karnataka Public Libraries Act?

(a) 1964 (b) 1965 (c) 1966

1202. What was the nomenclature of State Central Library of Karnataka in 1966?

(a) State Central Library

(b) State Central Reference Library

(c) Central State Library

1203. Where was the first Public Library established in 1854 in M.P.?

(a) Gwalior (b) Indore (c) Ujjain

1204. In which year was the Central Library of Gwalior established as Royal Govt. Library?

(a) 1925 (b) 1926 (c) 1927

1205. Which was the first commission in India which recommended the status of a librarian at par with professor and an ex-officio member of the Academic Council during 1917-19?

(a) Bombay (b) Calcutta (c) Delhi

1206. How many specialist classification schemes have been designed by the Classification Research Group, London?

(a) 21 (b) 22 (c) 25

1207. Which CAS service has been started for mentally retarded persons in Jan. 1986 from Secunderabad?

(a) CAS List (b) MENTARD
(c) MENTARD Bulletin

1208. When was Imperial Secretariat Library established?

(a) 1890 (b) 1891 (c) 1892

1209. In which year was Imperial Library (Indenture Validation) Act passed for public?

(a) 1901 (b) 1902 (c) 1903

1210. Who were allowed to consult the Imperial Library?

(a) Indian Citizens below 18 years

(b) Indian Citizens of 18 years

(c) Indian Citizens of 18 years and above

1211. How much was the collection of National Library as on March 31, 1990?

(a) 19,74,031 books (b) 19,74,000 books
(c) 19,74,025 books

1212. Which library is a nucleus of the Central Medical Library?

(a) Library of AIIMS

(b) Library of Indian Medical Association

(c) Library of Directorate General of Health Services

1213. Which index is published by Central Medical Library?
   (a) *Indian Medical Index*
   (b) *Index to Indian Medical Periodicals*
   (c) *Indian Medical Periodical*

1214. Which online Access to Databases is served by National Medical Library?
   (a) NMLINE (b) MEDLINE (c) MEDILINE

1215. Who is the publisher of *Bibliography of Indian Agriculture*, since 1944?
   (a) IARI Library
   (b) ICAR Library
   (c) Pantnagar Agriculture University

1216. Which publication is done for monthly clippings service in Agri-field?
   (a) News in Agriculture
   (b) Development News in Agriculture
   (c) Clipping News in Agriculture

1217. Who is publishing *The Archreion* from New Delhi?
   (a) Delhi Public Library
   (b) National Archives of India
   (c) Archaeological Survey of India

1218. Which Database is introduced in 1989 by INSDOC, available for online searching?
   (a) Current contents of journals
   (b) Current contents of Indian journals
   (c) Current contents of journals of India

1219. Which Database was started in 1972 by INSDOC?
   (a) Database of Polymer Science
   (b) Database of Indian Patents
   (c) Database of current journals

1220. INSDOC introduced in 1990, which of the following the databases?

(a) Database of Polymer Science

(b) Database of Indian Patents

(c) Polymer Science Database

1221. When did the Planning Commission Working Group on modernization of library services submit its report?

(a) 1980 (b) 1982 (c) 1984

1222. What term is used for a physical device found in the computer system?

(a) Software (b) Hardware (c) Operating System

1223. Which system is a programme used as a means of instructing computers to carry out operational tasks?

(a) Application Programme (b) Operating System
(c) Software Programme

1224. How many languages are categorized by Gilbert (1983)?

(a) Three (b) Four (c) Five

1225. Which title was conferred to Dr. S.R. Ranganathan by British Government in 1936?

(a) Ranga (b) Rao Sahib (c) Raoji

1226. Who called Dr. S.R. Ranganathan as the 'Father of the Library Science in India'?

(a) Sir Maurice Gwyer, V.C. of University of Delhi

(b) Dr. Bhagwati, V.C. of B.H.U.

(c) C.D. Deshmukh, Chairman, UGC, New Delhi

1227. Who counted Dr. S.R. Ranganathan "among the immortals of our profession" in 1943?

(a) Sir Maurice Gwyer (b) B.C. Vickery
(c) B.I. Palmer

1228. Which organisation honoured Dr. S.R. Ranganathan by electing him as an Honorary Member in Sept. 1957?

(a) IFLA (b) FID (c) CRG

1229. Which association honoured Dr. S.R. Ranganathan as its Vice President for life in 1957?

(a) LA (b) ALA (c) ILA

1230. Who introduced 'Feature Headings' in documentation?

(a) V.C. Vickery (b) S.R. Ranganathan
(c) H.E. Bliss

1231. Which platform presented festschrift to S.R. Ranganathan in 1951 at Indore on his 60th year of age?

(a) IASLIC (b) UPLA (c) ILA

1232. Who elected silver jubilee of CCC of S.R. Ranganathan in 1959?

(a) ILA (b) PLA (c) DLA

1233. When did S.R. Ranganathan join 'London School of Librarianship' for his first training of Librarianship?

(a) Sept. 24, 1924 (b) Aug. 5, 1923
(c) Sept. 20, 1924

1234. Who was the teacher of S.R. Ranganathan in London School of Librarianship?

(a) W.C. Berwick Sayers (b) V.C. Vickery
(c) Melvil Dewey

1235. What was the duration of training of Librarianship at London School of Librarianship in 1924?

(a) Three months (b) Four months
(c) Six months

1236. When did S.R. Ranganathan prepare first sample schedule for different facts and experimented on synthesized numbers?

(a) March 1925 (b) April 1925
(c) May 1925

1237. When did S.R. Ranganathan deliver a course of lectures to the Diploma Students of Bombay University when Dr. P.M. Joshi was the Librarian at the University library?

(a) 1944 (b) 1945 (c) 1946

1238. Who was the founder teacher of Deptt. of Library Science of Delhi University?

(a) S.R. Ranganathan (b) P.N. Kaula
(c) Krishna Kumar

1239. When Dr. Ranganathan along with his student S. Parthasarthy left for U.S.A. on the invitation of Rockfeller Foundation?

(a) 1949 (b) 1950 (c) 1951

1240. Ranganathan was invited to U.S.A. to attend the International Conference on Scientific Information held in:

(a) New York (b) Washington (c) Michigan

1241. Which school did not recognize the principle of corporate authorship recommended by Panizzi?

(a) Dewey School (b) Ranganathan School
(c) German School

1242. Where was the meeting of working group for International Cooperation held in 1954?

(a) Spain (b) Moscow (c) Zagreb

1243. Who wrote/drafted the *Code of Cataloguing Rules—Author and Title* which was published by ALA in 1960?

(a) Annie Cutter (Charles) (b) S.R. Ranganathan
(c) Lubetzkey

1244. When were the 'Prussion Cataloguing Instructions' promulgated?

(a) May 10, 1899 (b) May 10, 1900
(c) May 10, 1898

1245. Who published *Bibliographical Handbook No. 7* in Paris in 1958?

(a) UNESCO (b) IFLA (c) ALA

1246. Who published *A Study of Current Bibliographies of National Official Publications* in Paris in 1958?

(a) UNESCO (b) IFLA (c) FID

1247. In which system are cards for Japanese material and cards for occidental material filed in Japan?
   (a) Chinese material filed phonetically and occidental material filed alphabetically
   (b) Chinese material filed alphabetically and occidental material filed phonetically
   (c) Neither of the above systems of filing followed

1248. Who published Nippon catalogue rules in 1942?
   (a) Young Librarian Association
   (b) Japan Librarian Association
   (c) ALA

1249. When was *Nippon Decimal Classification (NDC)* published for Japanese Libraries?
   (a) 1925 (b) 1927 (c) 1929

1250. Which library, is an origin of Modern Japanese Library, established in 1872?
   (a) Tokyo Library
   (b) National Diet Library
   (c) Neither of the above

1251. When was Japan Library Association organised?
   (a) 1891 (b) 1892 (c) 1893

1252. When were the first cataloguing rules for Japanese and Chinese books enacted?
   (a) 1892 (b) 1893 (c) 1894

1253. The first course of library training school of one year was started in:
   (a) 1912 (b) 1913 (c) 1914

1254. Young Librarians' Federation set up the Cataloguing Committee for compilation of cataloguing rules in:
   (a) 1925 (b) 1929 (c) 1935

1255. Which is a code for cataloguing rules published in 1943 on the recommendation of cataloguing committee?
   (a) JLA cataloguing rules
   (b) Nihon cataloguing rules
   (c) Nihon cataloguing code

1256. In which book of S.R. Ranganathan a rule-by-rule comparative study of five catalogue codes is defined?
   (a) Classified catalogue code
   (b) Headings and canons
   (c) Theory of library catalogue

1257. When was the Rome conference of FID/CA held?
   (a) 1950 (b) 1951 (c) 1952

1258. For which purpose was the Dorking conference organised in U.K. in 1957?
   (a) Cataloguing for information retrieval
   (b) Classification for information retrieval
   (c) Documentation work

1259. Who was the Chairman of ISI Committee on Documentation and Standardization of Library Terminology?
   (a) S.R. Ranganathan (b) T.S. Rajgopalan
   (c) B.S. Kesavan

1260. Who was the Chairman of the Sectional Committee on Library Building, Fittings and Furniture organised in 1958?
   (a) S.R. Ranganathan (b) T.S. Rajgopalan
   (c) Girja Kumar

1261. Who was the founder of Adyar Library opened on Dec. 28, 1886?
   (a) Col. Henry Steela Olcott
   (b) Captain Jerse Mitchel
   (c) Dr. Gravely

1262. In which book Dr. S.R. Ranganathan dealt with various aspects of adult education in India?

(a) Organisation of libraries
(b) Education for leisure
(c) Five laws of library science

1263. Who ascribed the book famine to three factors, namely paralysis of language, latency of authorship, and technological inadequacy, challenging the social education?

(a) S.R. Ranganathan (b) Maharaja of Baroda
(c) UNESCO

1264. B.I. Palmer and A.J. Wells acknowledged their gratitude by dedicating their book "Fundamentals of Library Classification" to:

(a) Melvil Dewey
(b) Dr. S. Radhakrishnan
(c) S.R. Ranganathan

1265. In which year S.R. Ranganathan wrote the book *Library Development Plan* which explained a well-planned library system in India?

(a) 1948 (b) 1949 (c) 1950

1266. Who made pioneering efforts for "Open Access" in U.K.?

(a) James Duff Brown (b) Library of Congress
(c) J.S. Mill

1267. Who was the first person who used the word 'bibliography' in his book *Bibliographia Parisiana* in 1645?

(a) L.J. De Saint Charles (b) Paul Otlet
(c) C.A. Cutter

1268. What do we call Conrad Gesner regarding the bibliography?

(a) A Bibliographer
(b) Father of Bibliography
(c) A man of Bibliography

1269. What is the specific feature that deals with analytical bibliography?

(a) Author description (b) Title description

(c) Public standarded description

(d) Physical description

1270. Why King of Kashmir 'King Buddshah' is famous in librarianship?

(a) For encouraging paper making

(b) For providing equipment for paper making

(c) For discouraging paper making

1271. Which bibliography includes the reading material of the nation, for the nation and by the nation?

(a) *Selective Bibliography* (b) *Union Catalogue*

(c) *National Bibliography*

1272. What is the periodicity of National Bibliography *Knizhnaia Letopis* of USSR?

(a) Monthly (b) Fortnightly

(c) Weekly (d) Quarterly

1273. What is the full name of BBIP in the field of bibliography?

(a) British Bibliography in Print

(b) British Broad-in-Print

(c) British Books-in-Print

1274. In which International Book List, UDC is used for arranging entries in main sequence?

(a) FID Book List (b) IFLA Book List

(c) UNESCO Book List (d) ASLIB Book List

1275. Who is the publisher of *Cumulative Book Index* published in U.S.A.?

(a) McGraw Hill, New York

(b) Whitaker, London

(c) H.W. Wilson, New York

(d) Macmillan, New Delhi

1276. How many languages are covered by 'Indian National Bibliography'?

(a) 11 languages (b) 13 languages
(c) 14 languages (d) 15 languages

1277. Which catalogue code is followed by British National Bibliography for arranging entries?

(a) ALA (b) CCC
(c) AACR-II (d) LC Cataloguing rules

1278. Who is the publisher of *Books in Print*?

(a) H.W. Wilson, New York (b) R.R. Bowker
(c) Library of Congress

1279. Andrew Carnegie was a:

(a) Classification expert (b) Library Scientist
(c) Librarian (d) Philanthropist

1280. The concept of 'Literary Warrant' was given by:

(a) S.R. Ranganathan (b) Wyndhem Hulme
(c) E.C. Richardson (d) W.C.B. Sayers

1281. MBO concept came into existence in:

(a) 1950 (b) 1960 (c) 1970 (d) 1940

1282. Who has advanced the demand and supply theory in Book Selection?

(a) L.R. McColvin (b) Melvil Dewey
(c) Goldsmith

1283. Who has formulated the principle of 'Best reading for the largest number at the least cost'?

(a) F. Durry (b) L.R. McColvin
(c) Melvil Dewey

1284. Who has quoted this statement "Library is an open door through which people can participate in all the accumulated wisdom of race"?

(a) Thomas Brary (b) Melvil Dewey
(c) S.R. Ranganathan

1285. How many order cards are prepared for each book for Book Selection procedures?
   (a) One card one book
   (b) Two card one book
   (c) Three card one book

1286. Which element darkens the colour of paper and destroys the brightness of the book?
   (a) Smoking and gas fumes (b) Theft
   (c) Rains

1287. Fungus which is harmful to books grows in:
   (a) Sunlight (b) Dampness or moisture
   (c) Dust

1288. Which insects are found in size between ¼″ × ¼″ and appear in shiny scale covering, and destroy binding?
   (a) Cockroaches (b) Silver fish
   (c) Fungus

1289. Which insect eats the paper of a book?
   (a) Fungus (b) Bookworm
   (c) Silver fish

1290. Which system is a process of pressing cloth, paper, etc. between rollers, for the purpose of smooth and glazed printing?
   (a) Galley proofing (b) Calendering
   (c) Building

1291. The books produced in the infancy of the art of printing, specially produced before 1500 A.D. are called
   (a) Incunabula (b) Manuscripts
   (c) Handbooks

1292. When was DESIDOC established?
   (a) 1965 (b) 1966 (c) 1967

1293. When was the National Book Development Board set up by Government of India?
   (a) 1965 (b) 1966 (c) 1967

1294. When was the Publication Division of Ministry of Information and Broadcasting, Govt. of India set up?

(a) 1940 (b) 1941 (c) 1943

1295. When was the Madras School Book Society established for publishing of school testbooks?

(a) 1815 (b) 1820 (c) 1822

1296. When was the UNESCO Public Library manifesto issued?

(a) 1945 (b) 1947 (c) 1949

1297. Who replaced the principle of a Command of Fayol by the principle of 'Directing'?

(a) Gullick (b) Urwick (c) Taylor

MISCELLANEOUS QUESTIONS

1298. Which of the following is true about the knowledge?

(a) Finite (b) Infinite
(c) Continuum (d) None of them

1299. Microfilms and CDs are categorized as:

(a) Macro thought (b) Micro thought
(c) Micro print (d) Micro form

1300. When known interacts with the knowee, it becomes:

(a) Knowledge (b) Decision
(c) Language

1301. IIT Library, Gauhati was established in:

(a) 1995-96 (b) 2001-02
(c) 2002-03 (d) 1999-2000

1302. What types of thoughts are embodied in articles of a journal?

(a) Macro thoughts (b) Micro thoughts
(c) Neither of them

1303. Dissemination of knowledge is known as:

(a) Books (b) CAS (c) Bibliography

1304. Which service provides the right information at right moment to the right reader in right way and time?

(a) Reference service

(b) Current awareness service

(c) Bibliographical service

1305. Conservation of knowledge only is a/an:

(a) Old concept (b) New concept
(c) Neither of them

1306. Chemical Abstract is a/an:

(a) Abstracting journal (b) Indexing journal
(c) Bibliography

1307. Trade journals are published by:

(a) Commercial Publications

(b) Research Societies

(c) Educational Institutions

1308. Which documents are formulated by agreement, authority and customs of sponsors to define a product, material, process, procedures, quality, performance of nomenclature, etc.?

(a) Patents (b) Standards
(c) Conference papers

1309. The person conducting documentation work is known as:

(a) Librarian (b) Information Scientist
(c) Documentalist

1310. Who was the Librarian of Smithsonian Institute in 1850?

(a) Joseph Henry (b) Conard Von Gesner
(c) Charles C. Jewit

1311. Paul Otlet & Henry La Fontain were the nationals of:

(a) Germany (b) Belgium (c) France

1312. Which prize was awarded to La Fontain in 1913?

(a) National Prize of Belgium

(b) Nobel Peace Prize

(c) Noble Library Prize

1313. Who delivered the introductory lecture in the conference at Brusells in 1955?

(a) Paul Otlet (b) Theodore Besterman
(c) Alexander King

1314. Where is the Headquarter of the Committee FID/ET for education and training?

(a) Denmark (b) Hungary (c) Poland

1315. When was a joint committee for cooperation organised between IFLA and FID?

(a) 1930 (b) 1938 (c) 1940

1316. For what purpose IMCE (International Meeting on Cataloguing Experts) was held in Copenhagen in 1969?

(a) ISBN (b) ISBD (c) ISSN

1317. In which city the international conference on the improvement of Bibliographical services was held in Nov. 1950?

(a) Berlin (b) Paris (c) London

1318. Which classification system is followed by INIS (International Nuclear Information System)?

(a) DC (b) CC (c) UDC

1319. Which type of subject headings were used by INIS?

(a) Sears' List (b) Library of Congress
(c) Chain Procedure (d) USAEC Sub-heading

ANSWERS—CLASSIFICATION

1. (a) 2. (a) 3. (a) 4. (b) 5. (a)
6. (b) 7. (a) 8. (c) 9. (a) 10. (a)
11. (b) 12. (a) 13. (a) 14. (c) 15. (b)
16. (b) 17. (a) 18. (a) 19. (a) 20. (b)
21. (c) 22. (c) 23. (c) 24. (c) 25. (a)
26. (c) 27. (c) 28. (b) 29. (a) 30. (b)
31. (b) 32. (b) 33. (a) 34. (c) 35. (b)

36. (a) 37. (c) 38. (c) 39. (c) 40. (b)
41. (a) 42. (b) 43. (b) 44. (b) 45. (a)
46. (c) 47. (c) 48. (b) 49. (c) 50. (c)
51. (a) 52. (c) 53. (a) 54. (b) 55. (c)
56. (c) 57. (c) 58. (b) 59. (c) 60. (c)
61. (c) 62. (a) 63. (c) 64. (b) 65. (c)
66. (b) 67. (b) 68. (b) 69. (a) 70. (a)
71. (a) 72. (a) 73. (b) 74. (b) 75. (b)
76. (b) 77. (a) 78. (c) 79. (b) 80. (b)
81. (a) 82. (c) 83. (a) 84. (c) 85. (b)
86. (b) 87. (c) 88. (a) 89. (b) 90. (c)
91. (b) 92. (c) 93. (b) 94. (b) 95. (b)
96. (d) 97. (b) 98. (d) 99. (a) 100. (c)
101. (c) 102. (c) 103. (c) 104. (c) 105. (d)
106. (c) 107. (c) 108. (a) 109. (c) 110. (b)
111. (d) 112. (b) 113. (b) 114. (c) 115. (c)
116. (c) 117. (c) 118. (a) 119. (a) 120. (a)
121. (c) 122. (c) 123. (c) 124. (a) 125. (b)
126. (a) 127. (b) 128. (b) 129. (c) 130. (b)
131. (c) 132. (a) 133. (c) 134. (c) 135. (c)
136. (a) 137. (a) 138. (c) 139. (c) 140. (a)
141. (c) 142. (c) 143. (c) 144. (c) 145. (c)
146. (b) 147. (c) 148. (b) 149. (a) 150. (a)
151. (a) 152. (b) 153. (a) 154. (b) 155. (a)
156. (b) 157. (a) 158. (c) 159. (a) 160. (a)
161. (a) 162. (b) 163. (a) 164. (b) 165. (b)
166. (b) 167. (a) 168. (c) 169. (a) 170. (c)
171. (b) 172. (b) 173. (b) 174. (c) 175. (b)
176. (c) 177. (b) 178. (b) 179. (b) 180. (b)
181. (a) 182. (a) 183. (c) 184. (b) 185. (c)
186. (c) 187. (b) 188. (c) 189. (b) 190. (b)

191. (b)	192. (b)	193. (a)	194. (b)	195. (d)
196. (a)	197. (c)	198. (b)	199. (c)	200. (a)
201. (c)	202. (d)	203. (b)	204. (c)	205. (b)
206. (b)	207. (a)	208. (b)	209. (c)	210. (a)
211. (a)	212. (a)	213. (a)	214. (c)	215. (c)
216. (a)	217. (b)	218. (a)	219. (c)	220. (b)
221. (b)	222. (c)	223. (b)	224. (c)	225. (b)
226. (d)	227. (b)	228. (b)	229. (b)	230. (c)
231. (b)	232. (d)	233. (c)	234. (c)	235. (b)
236. (a)	237. (a)	238. (c)	239. (c)	240. (c)
241. (b)	242. (a)	243. (b)	244. (a)	245. (b)
246. (b)	247. (c)	248. (b)	249. (a)	250. (a)
251. (d)	252. (b)	253. (d)	254. (b)	255. (b)
256. (c)	257. (d)	258. (c)	259. (c)	260. (b)
261. (a)	262. (b)	263. (a)	264. (a)	265. (d)
266. (d)	267. (c)	268. (b)	269. (d)	270. (b)
271. (b)	272. (d)	273. (d)	274. (a)	275. (d)
276. (a)	277. (a)	278. (d)	279. (a)	280. (b)
281. (a)	282. (b)	283. (d)	284. (d)	285. (b)
286. (a)	287. (a)	288. (d)	289. (b)	290. (d)
291. (d)	292. (b)	293. (a)	294. (d)	295. (b)
296. (d)	297. (b)	298. (d)	299. (a)	300. (b)
301. (a)	302. (d)	303. (a)	304. (a)	305. (b)
306. (a)	307. (b)	308. (c)	309. (b)	310. (c)
311. (c)	312. (c)	313. (d)	314. (b)	315. (d)
316. (a)	317. (d)	318. (a)	319. (a)	320. (b)
321. (c)	322. (b)	323. (a)	324. (b)	325. (c)
326. (c)	327. (c)	328. (b)	329. (a)	330. (c)
331. (b)	332. (c)	333. (c)	334. (c)	335. (a)
336. (b)	337. (c)	338. (c)	339. (c)	340. (c)
341. (a)	342. (c)	343. (b)	344. (b)	345. (c)
346. (c)	347. (b)	348. (c)	349. (a)	350. (b)

351. (c)	352. (c)	353. (c)	354. (c)	355. (a)
356. (b)	357. (a)	358. (b)	359. (b)	360. (c)
361. (a)	362. (a)	363. (b)	364. (a)	365. (c)
366. (b)	367. (a)	368. (a)	369. (b)	370. (c)
371. (a)	372. (a)	373. (b)	374. (a)	375. (b)
376. (a)	377. (a)	378. (c)	379. (a)	380. (c)
381. (a)	382. (a)	383. (a)	384. (b)	385. (c)
386. (a)	387. (a)	388. (a)	389. (b)	390. (a)
391. (b)	392. (c)	393. (a)	394. (a)	395. (b)
396. (b)	397. (a)	398. (a)	399. (c)	400. (a)
401. (c)	402. (c)	403. (b)	404. (a)	405. (b)
406. (b)	407. (a)	408. (a)	409. (a)	410. (c)
411. (c)	412. (c)	413. (c)	414. (c)	415. (a)
416. (c)	417. (c)	418. (b)	419. (a)	420. (c)
421. (b)	422. (b)	423. (b)	424. (b)	425. (a)
426. (a)	427. (c)	428. (b)	429. (b)	430. (a)
431. (b)	432. (b)	433. (a)	434. (c)	435. (b)
436. (c)	437. (a)	438. (c)	439. (b)	440. (c)
441. (c)	442. (c)	443. (c)	444. (a)	445. (c)
446. (b)	447. (a)	448. (a)	449. (a)	450. (a)
451. (a)	452. (c)	453. (a)	454. (a)	455. (a)
456. (c)	457. (a)	458. (b)	459. (c)	460. (b)
461. (a)	462. (a)	463. (b)	464. (b)	465. (d)
466. (c)	467. (b)	468. (a)	469. (c)	470. (c)
471. (a)	472. (a)	473. (a)	474. (c)	475. (b)
476. (a)	477. (a)	478. (c)	479. (a)	480. (b)
481. (a)	482. (a)	483. (b)	484. (a)	485. (c)
486. (a)	487. (a)	488. (a)	489. (a)	490. (a)
491. (c)	492. (b)	493. (a)	494. (a)	495. (a)
496. (a)	497. (a)	498. (a)	499. (a)	500. (a)
501. (b)	502. (a)	503. (b)	504. (b)	505. (b)

506. (b)	507. (c)	508. (b)	509. (a)	510. (c)
511. (b)	512. (b)	513. (b)	514. (b)	515. (a)
516. (b)	517. (c)	518. (b)	519. (a)	520. (a)
521. (b)	522. (a)	523. (b)	524. (a)	525. (c)
526. (c)	527. (c)	528. (d)	529. (c)	530. (b)
531. (b)	532. (a)	533. (c)	534. (d)	535. (c)
536. (c)	537. (c)	538. (c)	539. (b)	540. (b)
541. (b)	542. (b)	543. (b)	544. (a)	545. (a)
546. (c)	547. (d)	548. (c)	549. (d)	550. (d)
551. (b)	552. (a)	553. (c)	554. (a)	555. (c)
556. (c)	557. (d)	558. (b)	559. (a)	560. (d)
561. (b)	562. (b)	563. (c)	564. (c)	565. (b)
566. (a)	567. (c)	568. (d)	569. (d)	570. (c)
571. (c)	572. (b)	573. (c)	574. (b)	575. (c)
576. (d)	577. (c)	578. (a)	579. (a)	580. (d)
581. (b)	582. (a)	583. (c)	584. (b)	585. (b)
586. (b)	587. (b)	588. (b)	589. (b)	590. (b)
591. (a)	592. (a)	593. (a)	594. (a)	595. (a)
596. (a)	597. (a)	598. (b)	599. (c)	600. (c)
601. (b)	602. (c)	603. (c)	604. (b)	605. (c)
606. (c)	607. (c)	608. (a)	609. (c)	610. (c)
611. (c)	612. (c)	613. (c)	614. (b)	615. (c)
616. (c)	617. (c)	618. (c)	619. (c)	620. (b)
621. (b)	622. (c)	623. (c)	624. (a)	625. (c)
626. (c)	627. (c)	628. (c)	629. (b)	630. (a)
631. (a)	632. (c)	633. (d)	634. (c)	635. (d)
636. (b)	637. (c)	638. (d)	639. (c)	640. (b)
641. (b)	642. (c)	643. (c)	644. (c)	645. (c)
646. (a)	647. (b)	648. (c)	649. (c)	650. (c)
651. (c)	652. (d)	653. (a)	654. (c)	655. (b)
656. (b)	657. (c)	658. (c)	659. (b)	660. (a)

661. (c)	662. (c)	663. (d)	664. (c)	665. (b)
666. (b)	667. (c)	668. (c)	669. (b)	670. (b)
671. (a)	672. (b)	673. (c)	674. (c)	675. (a)
676. (a)	677. (d)	678. (c)	679. (c)	680. (c)
681. (b)	682. (b)	683. (c)	684. (d)	685. (b)
686. (c)	687. (c)	688. (c)	689. (d)	690. (c)
691. (c)	692. (c)	693. (c)	694. (b)	695. (c)
696. (b)	697. (b)	698. (a)	699. (b)	700. (b)
701. (b)	702. (d)	703. (b)	704. (c)	705. (b)
706. (b)	707. (b)	708. (a)	709. (c)	710. (a)
711. (c)	712. (b)	713. (b)	714. (c)	715. (b)
716. (c)	717. (b)	718. (c)	719. (c)	720. (b)
721. (b)	722. (c)	723. (c)	724. (b)	725. (c)
726. (b)	727. (a)	728. (c)	729. (c)	730. (c)
731. (c)	732. (d)	733. (c)	734. (b)	735. (a)
736. (a)	737. (d)	738. (b)	739. (d)	740. (b)
741. (c)	742. (c)	743. (d)	744. (d)	745. (c)
746. (a)	747. (b)	748. (d)	749. (b)	750. (c)
751. (b)	752. (a)	753. (b)	754. (a)	755. (b)
756. (c)	757. (c)	758. (c)	759. (c)	760. (a)
761. (a)	762. (d)	763. (a)	764. (a)	765. (a)
766. (b)	767. (b)	768. (a)	769. (a)	770. (b)
771. (a)	772. (a)	773. (b)	774. (c)	775. (a)
776. (a)	777. (a)	778. (a)	779. (c)	780. (c)
781. (c)	782. (c)	783. (d)	784. (b)	785. (c)
786. (b)	787. (c)	788. (c)	789. (a)	790. (a)
791. (b)	792. (a)	793. (c)	794. (a)	795. (d)
796. (d)	797. (a)	798. (c)	799. (b)	800. (a)
801. (d)	802. (c)	803. (c)	804. (a)	805. (d)
806. (d)	807. (b)	808. (a)	809. (d)	810. (c)
811. (c)	812. (c)	813. (d)	814. (b)	815. (a)

816. (a)	817. (c)	818. (d)	819. (d)	820. (b)
821. (b)	822. (a)	823. (b)	824. (c)	825. (a)
826. (b)	827. (c)	828. (a)	829. (a)	830. (d)
831. (c)	832. (c)	833. (d)	834. (c)	835. (a)
836. (b)	837. (c)	838. (d)	839. (d)	840. (d)
841. (c)	842. (b)	843. (d)	844. (d)	845. (c)
846. (b)	847. (c)	848. (a)	849. (b)	850. (a)
851. (a)	852. (c)	853. (a)	854. (b)	855. (b)
856. (b)	857. (c)	858. (c)	859. (c)	860. (c)
861. (c)	862. (c)	863. (c)	864. (c)	865. (a)
866. (c)	867. (a)	868. (c)	869. (b)	870. (a)
871. (b)	872. (b)	873. (c)	874. (c)	875. (c)
876. (b)	877. (c)	878. (c)	879. (b)	880. (c)
881. (a)	882. (a)	883. (a)	884. (b)	885. (b)
886. (a)	887. (c)	888. (b)	889. (a)	890. (d)
891. (d)	892. (a)	893. (c)	894. (d)	895. (b)
896. (b)	897. (b)	898. (c)	899. (b)	900. (a)
901. (b)	902. (b)	903. (c)	904. (c)	905. (c)
906. (c)	907. (c)	908. (b)	909. (c)	910. (b)
911. (c)	912. (b)	913. (c)	914. (c)	915. (a)
916. (a)	917. (b)	918. (c)	919. (c)	920. (c)
921. (a)	922. (b)	923. (a)	924. (b)	925. (c)
926. (b)	927. (c)	928. (a)	929. (c)	930. (b)
931. (a)	932. (a)	933. (a)	934. (b)	935. (a)
936. (a)	937. (a)	938. (b)	939. (b)	940. (b)
941. (a)	942. (a)	943. (a)	944. (a)	945. (c)
946. (a)	947. (b)	948. (b)	949. (b)	950. (a)
951. (c)	952. (b)	953. (c)	954. (c)	955. (b)
956. (c)	957. (a)	958. (c)	959. (b)	960. (a)
961. (b)	962. (b)	963. (c)	964. (c)	965. (a)
966. (c)	967. (a)	968. (b)	969. (c)	970. (a)

971. (a)	972. (c)	973. (c)	974. (c)	975. (c)
976. (c)	977. (b)	978. (a)	979. (b)	980. (b)
981. (c)	982. (b)	983. (b)	984. (c)	985. (b)
986. (b)	987. (b)	988. (c)	989. (c)	990. (c)
991. (b)	992. (c)	993. (c)	994. (c)	995. (c)
996. (b)	997. (c)	998. (b)	999. (d)	1000. (b)
1001. (c)	1002. (b)	1003. (d)	1004. (b)	1005. (b)
1006. (a)	1007. (b)	1008. (b)	1009. (b)	1010. (b)
1011. (b)	1012. (a)	1013. (b)	1014. (a)	1015. (b)
1016. (b)	1017. (a)	1018. (a)	1019. (a)	1020. (c)
1021. (c)	1022. (b)	1023. (a)	1024. (b)	1025. (c)
1026. (a)	1027. (b)	1028. (c)	1029. (b)	1030. (c)
1031. (a)	1032. (b)	1033. (b)	1034. (b)	1035. (b)
1036. (c)	1037. (a)	1038. (a)	1039. (c)	1040. (a)
1041. (a)	1042. (b)	1043. (d)	1044. (c)	1045. (a)
1046. (b)	1047. (a)	1048. (b)	1049. (c)	1050. (a)
1051. (c)	1052. (a)	1053. (b)	1054. (c)	1055. (a)
1056. (b)	1057. (b)	1058. (c)	1059. (a)	1060. (c)
1061. (c)	1062. (b)	1063. (a)	1064. (c)	1065. (c)
1066. (b)	1067. (a)	1068. (c)	1069. (d)	1070. (b)
1071. (b)	1072. (b)	1073. (a)	1074. (b)	1075. (b)
1076. (b)	1077. (b)	1078. (b)	1079. (b)	1080. (c)
1081. (b)	1082. (b)	1083. (b)	1084. (a)	1085. (a)
1086. (b)	1087. (b)	1088. (b)	1089. (c)	1090. (c)
1091. (d)	1092. (d)	1093. (c)	1094. (b)	1095. (c)
1096. (b)	1097. (c)	1098. (b)	1099. (b)	1100. (c)
1101. (c)	1102. (b)	1103. (b)	1104. (b)	1105. (c)
1106. (b)	1107. (a)	1108. (c)	1109. (b)	1110. (b)
1111. (d)	1112. (c)	1113. (c)	1114. (a)	1115. (c)
1116. (c)	1117. (d)	1118. (b)	1119. (b)	1120. (a)
1121. (c)	1122. (c)	1123. (c)	1124. (c)	1125. (b)

1126. (d)	1127. (b)	1128. (b)	1129. (b)	1130. (b)
1131. (c)	1132. (c)	1133. (b)	1134. (a)	1135. (c)
1136. (a)	1137. (c)	1138. (d)	1139. (d)	1140. (b)
1141. (c)	1142. (b)	1143. (a)	1144. (a)	1145. (a)
1146. (c)	1147. (b)	1148. (b)	1149. (b)	1150. (b)
1151. (c)	1152. (b)	1153. (d)	1154. (b)	1155. (b)
1156. (a)	1157. (a)	1158. (b)	1159. (a)	1160. (a)
1161. (b)	1162. (d)	1163. (b)	1164. (b)	1165. (c)
1166. (d)	1167. (a)	1168. (b)	1169. (a)	1170. (c)
1171. (a)	1172. (a)	1173. (b)	1174. (a)	1175. (b)
1176. (c)	1177. (c)	1178. (c)	1179. (c)	1180. (b)
1181. (c)	1182. (b)	1183. (b)	1184. (a)	1185. (a)
1186. (a)	1187. (c)	1188. (c)	1189. (a)	1190. (c)
1191. (b)	1192. (a)	1193. (b)	1194. (c)	1195. (a)
1196. (c)	1197. (c)	1198. (b)	1199. (b)	1200. (b)
1201. (a)	1202. (b)	1203. (b)	1204. (b)	1205. (c)
1206. (b)	1207. (b)	1208. (c)	1209. (b)	1210. (c)
1211. (c)	1212. (a)	1213. (c)	1214. (b)	1215. (b)
1216. (a)	1217. (b)	1218. (b)	1219. (b)	1220. (b)
1221. (c)	1222. (c)	1223. (b)	1224. (b)	1225. (c)
1226. (b)	1227. (a)	1228. (c)	1229. (b)	1230. (a)
1231. (b)	1232. (c)	1233. (c)	1234. (a)	1235. (a)
1236. (a)	1237. (a)	1238. (a)	1239. (a)	1240. (b)
1241. (b)	1242. (c)	1243. (c)	1244. (c)	1245. (a)
1246. (a)	1247. (a)	1248. (a)	1249. (a)	1250. (c)
1251. (a)	1252. (b)	1253. (b)	1254. (a)	1255. (b)
1256. (b)	1257. (b)	1258. (b)	1259. (b)	1260. (a)
1261. (a)	1262. (a)	1263. (b)	1264. (a)	1265. (c)
1266. (c)	1267. (a)	1268. (a)	1269. (b)	1270. (a)
1271. (a)	1272. (c)	1273. (c)	1274. (c)	1275. (d)
1276. (c)	1277. (c)	1278. (c)	1279. (b)	1280. (d)

1281. (a) 1282. (c) 1283. (a) 1284. (a) 1285. (a)
1286. (a) 1287. (a) 1288. (b) 1289. (b) 1290. (b)
1291. (b) 1292. (a) 1293. (c) 1294. (c) 1295. (b)
1296. (b) 1297. (c) 1298. (a) 1299. (b) 1300. (d)
1301. (b) 1302. (c) 1303. (b) 1304. (b) 1305. (b)
1306. (b) 1307. (a) 1308. (a) 1309. (b) 1310. (c)
1311. (c) 1312. (b) 1313. (b) 1314. (c) 1315. (c)
1316. (b) 1317. (b) 1318. (b) 1319. (c)

Appendices

***Appendix* I**

LIFETIME OF LIBRARY PROFESSIONAL

1.	M. Tanbe	-	1910-1965
2.	K.F.O. Dziatzko	-	1842-1903
3.	Anthony Panizzi	-	1797-1879
4.	W.C. Berwick Sayers	-	1881-1960
5.	S.C. Bradford	-	1878-1948
6.	E.C. Richardson	-	1860-1939
7.	Fremont Rider	-	1885-1962
8.	J.D. Brown	-	1862-1914
9.	Melvil Dewey	-	1851-1931
10.	Dr. S.R. Ranganathan	-	1892-1972
11.	H.E. Bliss	-	1870-1955
12.	C.A. Cutter	-	1837-1903
13.	A. Carnegie		1835-1919
14.	Edward Edwards	-	1812-1886

FULL NAME OF LIBRARY PROFESSIONALS

1.	L.S. Jast	-	Louis Stanlay Jastzebski
2.	S.C. Bradford	-	Samuel Clement Bradford
3.	E.C. Richardson	-	Ernest Abbert Savage
4.	Paul Otlet	-	Paul Marie-Ghislain Otlet
5.	B.S. Kesavan	-	Bellary Shamanna Kesavan
6.	B.I. Palmer	-	Bernard Ira Palmer
7.	L.R. McColvin	-	Lionel Roy Mc Colvin
8.	Fremont Rider	-	Arthur Fremont Rider
9.	A Neelameghan	-	Arashanapalai Neelamaghan
10.	C.G. Vishwanathan	-	Caduveti Gurusubrahmanya Vishwanathan
11.	W.F. Poole	-	William Frederick Poole
12.	H.E. Bliss	-	Henry Evelyn Bliss
13.	D.J. Foskett	-	Douglas John Foskett
14.	J. Mills	-	Jack Mills
15.	D.N. Marshall	-	Dora Nusserwanji Marshall
16.	M.E. Sears	-	Minnie Earl Sears

ARTICLES

Arabic	:	ad, al, ar, as, at, eg
Dutch	:	de, het, t, een, cene
English	:	a, an, the
French	:	le, la, les, un, une
German	:	das, den, die, ein, eine
Hebrew	:	ha, he
Hungarian	:	a, az, egy
Italian	:	gli, gl, i, il, l', la, le, lo, un, una, uno
Portuguese	:	a, as, o, un, uma
Scandinavian	:	de, den, det, en, et, ett
Spanish	:	el, la, lo, los, un, una
Yiddish	:	der, di, dos

CONTRACTORS

Abridge	:	Abr
Annotated	:	Annot
Assistant	:	Assis
Author(s)	:	Auth
Before Christ	:	BC
Century	:	Cent
Commentary	:	Comm
Commentator	:	Comm
Compiled	:	Comp
Dedication(s)	:	Ded
Director	:	Dir
Editor(s)	:	Ed
Fascicule	:	Fasc
Illustration	:	Ill
Introduction	:	Introd
Joint	:	Jt
Number(s)	:	No
Preface	:	Pref
Pseudonym	:	Pseud
Report	:	Rep
Revised	:	Rev
Special	:	Sp
Translated	:	Tr
Volume(s)	:	V

APPENDIX 2

Publication of DDC (Printed by Forest Press, New York)

Ed.	Year	Page	Copies	Editor
1.	1876	44	1000	Melvil Dewey
2.	1885	314	500	Melvil Dewey & W.S. Biscoe
3.	1888	416	500	Melvil Dewey & W.S. Biscoe
4.	1891	466	500	May Seymour
5.	1894	467	1000	May Seymour
6.	1899	511	7600	May Seymour
7.	1911	792	2000	May Seymour
8.	1913	850	2000	May Seymour
9.	1915	856	3000	May Seymour
10.	1919	940	4000	May Seymour
11.	1922	944	5000	Dorkas Fellows
12.	1927	1243	9340	Dorkas Fellows
13.	1932	1647	9750	Dorkas Fellows & M.W. Gelchell
14.	1942	1927	15632	Constantin Mazney & M.W. Gelchell
15.	1951	716	11200	Milton J. Ferguson
15th rev.	1952	927	11045	Godfrey Dewey
16.	1958	2439	31011	Banjamin A. Cluster & D., Haykin
17th rev. index	1965	2153	38677	Benjamin A. Cluster
18.	1971	2718	NA	Benjamin A. Cluster
19.	1979	3361	NA	Benjamin A. Cluster
20.	1989	NA	NA	Benjamin A. Cluster
21.	1998	NA	NA	Benjamin A. Cluster

Services/ Databases available on Internet/WWW

	Database	Compiled/Sponsored
1.	Viruses (Osmond database)	Dr. Cornelia B. Osmond
2.	India World (RDC)	Ravi Database
3.	World Cup Cricket 1996 (PMG and RDC)	Professional Management Group and Ravi Database
4.	World of Planets	NASA, U.S.A.
5.	Ayurvedic Treatment	P.S. Chauhan
6.	Newspapers, Magazines & Journals	*The Hindu*
7.	Vedas	Jivanet
8.	DDC/Dewey Home Page	OCLC (Forest Press, U.S.A.)
9.	Atlanta Olympics (1996)	IBM
10.	Marriage Bureau Matrimonial Service Site	PANALINK (Delhi)
11.	American Rarebooks (1775-1850)	University of Virginia
12.	Mother Teresa	Bab Bernatcin
13.	Jain Commission Report on Rajiv Gandhi Assassination	*India Index Magazine*
14.	Music plays	AIR and Doordarshan
15.	Bhartiya Janta Party	BJP

Videotex

1.	PRESTEL Videotex system (view data service) (Britain : 1978)	960 characters in 1200 bit/s 24 rows × by 40 Column array
2.	Antiope videotex (Teletex system) (French : 1981)	Each character 2400 bit/s is defined by 16 bits (40 rows)
3.	Teledom Videotex (Teletex system) (Canada : 1980)	Picture composed uses upto 1000,000 cells through normal TV
4.	Captain Videotex system (Telephone Access Inf. Network) (Japan : 1983)	192 rows × 240 columns 4800 bit/s
5.	Oracle (ITALY, U.K. : 1974)	200 pages on TV Screen (920 characters)
6.	Captain Videotex System (view data service) (Japan : 1987)	TV screen 24 lines

Some Machines Readable Database
(Suitable for CAS service)

1.	Books in Print	R.R. Bowker	Through online search services
2.	Books in print-plus	R.R. Bowker	CD-ROM version
3.	Any book (1988)	Library cooperation	Micro-computer based CD-ROM system
4.	Acquisition system from OCLC	OCLC	IBM compatible Micro computer system
5.	Bibliographical data-based system	M/s Small Library Computing	-do-
6.	Acquisition Serials Control System	M/s Innovative Interfaces Inc.	Turnkey System
7.	LIBS product line	CLSI	Minicomputer based
8.	Atlas system	Data Research Asso.	-do-
9.	The NOTIS software package	North Western Univ.	-do-
10.	LIBIS Software package	IBM	-do-
11.	TECHLIB/STATS	Info-dimensions	-do-
12.	Data system software package	Backer & Tayler	LIBRIS-II Computer based
13.	OLAS online ordering system	Brodart	For bibliographical work

Growth of Satellite Technology in India (In Chronological order)

	Rocket	Satellite	Purpose	Date	Result
1.	SLV-3	Rohini	Earth	10.08.79	Failure
2.	Observation SLV-3	Rohini	Earth	18.07.80	Success
3.	Observation SLV-3	Rohini	Scientific	31.05.81	Failure
4.	SLV-3	Rohini	Scientific	17.04.83	Success
5.	ASLV-D1	Scross-I	Technology	24.03.87	Failure
6.	ASLV-D2	Scross-II	Technology	13.07.88	Failure
7.	ASLV-D3	Scross-III	Scientific	20.05.92	Success
8.	PSLV-D1	IRS-IE	Remote sensing	20.09.93	Failure
9.	ASLV-D4	IRS	Scientific	04.05.94	Success
10.	PSLV-D2	IRS-P2	Remote sensing	15.09.94	Success
11.	PSLV-D3	IRS-P3	Remote sensing	21.03.96	Success
12.	PSLV-C1	IRS-ID	Remote sensing	29.09.97	Success

(*The Indian Express* : 01.01.97)

Software Package for Automatic Circulation Control

1.	NOTIS Software	Runsoul BB Mainframe
2.	DOBIS? LIBIS	Runsoul BB Mainframe
3.	PALS	Runsoul on Unisys
4.	LIAS	Runsoul Honeywell computers
5.	Constrows Bibliotech System	Digital Equipments VAX
6.	VTLS and Index System	Howlett Packard HP-3000

Services available on Internet

(a) *Services offered*:

  (i) E-mail / Bulletin Board
  (ii) FTP (File Transfer Protocol)
  (iii) Telnet (remote sensing facilities)
  (iv) Electronic publishing using WWW

(b) *Services made available on Internet*:

  (i) WWW (World Wide Web)
  (ii) Gropher
  (iii) Internet-Relay Chart (IRC)
  (iv) Usenet News Groups
  (v) Remote log-in to the host computer
  (vi) Archie
  (vii) Mosaic

(c) *Network connected with Internet*:

  (i) SIRNET (INSDOC)
  (ii) NICNET (Connecting 150 countries)
  (iii) INDONET (CMC Ltd.)

(d) *Private firms connected with Internet*:

  (i) Mahindras
  ii) Wipro Infotech
  (iii) Datapro
  (iv) Sprint RPG (Delhi)

(e) *Internet Supporting Software*:

  (i) Windows 95 (OS) and Plus (Microsoft Corp. U.S.A.)
  (ii) Browser (Netscape Communication Corp.)
  (iii) Java Script (Sun Micro System & Netscape jointly)
  (iv) Netcruiser (1.6) Netcom

Optical CD-ROM Technology—(at a glance)

OCR Functions Step (Input)	Store device medium	Transmission	Printing/ Output
1. Document Transport	1. Laser optical disk	1. Optical fibre	1. Optical electrostatic printer
(a) Individual Doc.	(a) Read-Only optical disk	2. Others	2. Laser printer
(b) Continuous roll			
2. Scanning	(b) WORM (Write once read many)		3. Optical font
(a) CCD Scanner			4. High resolution video monitor
(b) Laser Scanner	(c) EOD (Write table and erasable optical disk)		
(c) DOC Scanner			
(d) Matrix-Matching Device			
(e) Feature Extraction Device	2. Optical Card		
	3. Optical Tape		
3. Recognition			
(a) Mark-sense Recognition			
(b) Barcode-label Recognition			
4. Reading sensing			
(a) Optical			
(b) Page reader			
(c) Character reader			
(d) Optical sensor			

Constitution of Classified Catalogue Code

Part A	-	5 chapters describe the evolution of code.
Part B	-	9 chapters expound the canons of cataloguing.
Part C	-	7 chapters deal with five laws of Library Science.
Part D	-	7 chapters deal with evolution of the library catalogue in its internal and external form.
Part E	-	5 chapters deal with evolution of Library Catalogue.
Part F	-	17 chapters deal with the establishment of a standard terminology.
Part G	-	5 chapters deal with determination of the author of document.
Part H	-	7 chapters deals with the structure of name of persons in different cultural groups.
Part J	-	8 chapters prescribe the rules of rendering different kinds of names—persons, geographical, corporate and also names of books and series.
Part K	-	12 chapters develop the technique of chain procedure.
Part L	-	6 chapters deal with the cross reference index entries.
Part M	-	11 chapters of part M form the core of the book.
Part N	-	3 chapters give the supplementary rules for composit book and multivolume book.
Part P	-	11 chapters analyse the complexities normally met in periodical publications.
Part Q to V	-	44 chapters give additional rules necessary in building a Union Catalogue of books.